WBI LEARNING RESOURCES SERIES

Economic Development
and
Environmental Sustainability

Policies and Principles for a Durable Equilibrium

Edited by

José I. dos R. Furtado
and
Tamara Belt
with

Ramachandra Jammi

The World Bank
Washington, D. C.

The World Bank Institute (incorporating the former Economic Development Institute (EDI)/Learning and Leadership Center) was established by the World Bank in 1955 to train officials concerned with development planning, policymaking, investment analysis, and project implementation in member developing countries. At present the substance of the WBI's work emphasizes macroeconomic and sectoral economic policy analysis. Through a variety of courses, seminars, and workshops, most of which are given overseas in cooperation with local institutions, the WBI seeks to sharpen analytical skills used in policy analysis and to broaden understanding of the experience of individual countries with economic development. Although the WBI's publications are designed to support its training activities, many are of interest to a much broader audience.

José I. dos R. Furtado is senior environmental specialist in the Environment and Natural Resources Division of the World Bank Institute.
Tamara Belt is an environmental economist at the Inter-American Development Bank.
Ramachandra Jammi is a consultant in the Environment and Natural Resources Division of the World Bank Institute. .

Library of Congress Cataloging-in-Publication Data

Economic Development and Environmental Sustainability / Jose I. Dos R. Furtado,
Tamara Belt.
    p. cm.—(WBI learning resources series)
  The book is based on seminars conducted by the World Bank Institute in collaboration
with the Foundation for Advanced Studies on International Development, Japan.
  Includes bibliographical references (p.   ).
  ISBN 0-8213-4573-7

    1. Sustainable development—Congresses. 2. Economic development—Environmental
aspects—Congresses. 3. Environmental policy. I. Furtado, J. I.   II. Belt, Tamara.
III. Series.

HD75.6.E2946   2000
333.7—dc21

                                                        99-041173

Contents

Foreword   *vii*

Acknowledgments   *ix*

1. Economic Development and Environmental Sustainability: An Overview   *1*
   Economic Development and the Environment   *1*
   Organization of the Book   *1*

2. Policy Implications for Sustainable Development   *7*
   Human Society and the Environment   *7*
   Sustainable Development   *8*
   Policy Recommendations for Sustainable Development   *11*
   Conclusion   *14*
   Appendix 1. Rio Declaration on Environment and Development   *14*
   Appendix 2. Agenda 21, Chapter 1   *18*

3. Ecological Basis of Environmental Sustainability   *21*
   Sustainability from the Ecological Perspective   *21*
   Policy Implications of the Axioms   *28*
   Conclusion   *29*

4. The Dynamics of Creating and Maintaining Wealth   *31*
   Expanded Wealth Accounts   *31*
   Eco-Domestic Product   *32*
   Genuine Savings   *33*
   Social Capital   *35*
   Integrating Genuine Savings, Human Capital, and Social Capital into Policy   *38*
   Conclusion   *38*

5. Institutions for Environmental Stewardship   *41*
   Developing the Knowledge Base   *41*
   Setting Priorities   *42*
   Building Consensus   *42*
   Promoting Coordination   *42*
   Carrying out Implementation   *43*
   Involving Local People   *44*
   Conclusion   *46*

6. Poverty, Income Distribution, and the Environment   *49*
   Links between Poverty and the Environment: The Mainstream View   *49*
   Links between Poverty and the Environment: An Alternative View   *52*
   Conclusion   *53*

7. Population, Natural Resources, and the Environment   *57*
   Trends in Population Growth   *57*
   The Links between Population and Environment   *58*
   Population and Consumption Patterns   *60*
   Policy Recommendations   *64*
   Conclusion   *65*

8. Energy Consumption and the Environment   *67*
   Energy Use   *67*
   Policy Options   *70*
   Conclusion   *72*

9. Trade and the Environment   *75*
   Links among Trade, Economics, and the Environment   *75*
   General Agreement on Tariffs and Trade, World Trade Organization,
     and Environmental Management   *78*
   Policy Implications of Trade and the Environment   *79*
   Conclusion   *81*

10. Global Environmental Issues   *83*
    Developing Markets for Global Issues   *84*
    International Transfer of Funds   *86*
    International Agreements and Conventions   *87*
    National Policy for Global Issues   *90*
    Conclusion   *91*

11. Human Health and the Environment   *93*
    Household Environment   *93*
    Occupational Environment   *96*
    Ambient Environment   *96*
    Measuring and Valuing Environmental Effects on Health   *97*
    Priority Setting for Policymaking   *99*
    Conclusion   *100*
    Appendix: Disability-Adjusted Life Year   *100*

12. Planning and Environmental Indicators   *105*
    Measuring Progress toward Sustainability   *105*
    Indicators   *107*
    Information Requirements   *109*
    Temporal and Spatial Dimensions of Indicators   *110*
    International and National Projects to Develop Indicators   *111*
    Conclusion   *111*
    Appendix: Sustainable Use of Natural Resources in Mountain Areas   *112*

Boxes
9.1   Environmental Regulations and Competitiveness   *80*
10.1   The Aral Sea Program   *85*
10.2   Creation of a Carbon Market   *88*
12.1   Criteria for Indicator Selection   *109*

Figures
2.1   The Relationship between the Socioeconomic System and the Environment   *7*
2.2   Optimality, Sustainability, and Survivability of Development   *10*
2.3   Mainstreaming Environmental Considerations: Examples of Actors and Actions   *13*
3.1   Interplay of Economic, Ecological, and Sociological Factors for Attaining
        Sustainable Development   *24*
3.2   Ecosystem Processes   *26*
3.3   Productivity Capacity of Different Types of Resources   *27*
4.1   Genuine Savings for Tunisia, 1970–94   *33*
4.2   Genuine Savings Rates by Region, 1970–94   *34*

5.1   Consensus Building in Environmental Management: The Role of the Public Sector
        and Civil Society   *45*
6.1   Breaking the Cycle of Poverty-Environment-Population Growth   *50*
7.1   World Population Projections under Different Fertility Trends, 1985–2160   *58*
7.2   Actual and Projected Population Growth Rates by Region, 1850–2025   *59*
7.3   Actual and Projected Rural and Urban Populations by Region and Income, 1960–2025   *60*
7.4   Links among Population, the Environment, and Poverty   *61*
7.5   Relationship between Forest Coverage and Population Density in
        60 Tropical Countries, 1980   *64*
8.1   Commercial Energy Consumption, 1988   *69*
9.1   Trade and the Environment   *76*
11.1 Population without Sanitation or Water Supply Services, Selected Countries
        and Regions, 1990   *95*
11.2 Approaches to Valuing the Environmental Impacts on Health   *98*
12.1 Indicators to Meet the Challenges of Sustainable Development   *106*
12.2 Aggregation of Data   *108*
12.3 Pressure-State-Response Framework   *108*
12.4 The Changing Nature of Environmental Problems   *110*

Tables
2.1   Functions and Services Provided by the Environment   *8*
2.2   Physical Account for Commercial Forests in France, 1969–79   *14*
3.1   Evolution of the Biosphere and Climate   *22*
4.1   Wealth by Geographic Region, 1994   *32*
4.2   Some Indicators of Social Capital   *36*
6.1   Gini Indexes, Selected Countries and Years   *51*
6.2   Possibilities for and Constraints to Reviving Traditional Resource Use Systems   *54*
7.1   Average Annual Resource Consumption Per Capita, Various Years   *62*
7.2   Population Growth and Energy Consumption by Region, Selected Years   *63*
7.3   Changes in Land Use by Selected Country and Region, 1850–1980   *63*
8.1   Energy Consumption by Selected Regions and Economies, 1994   *68*
10.1 Global Environmental Problems Broken Down by Type of Externality   *84*
10.2 GEF Operational Outputs by Type, Fiscal 1995–98   *87*
11.1 Different Types of Environments and Potential Risks to Human Health   *94*
11.A1 Estimated Global Burden of Disease from Selected Environmental Threats, 1990,
        and Potential Reductions through Environmental Interventions   *101*
11.A2 Estimated Burden of Disease from Poor Household Environments in Demographically
        Developing Countries, 1990, and Potential Reduction through Improved
        Household Services   *102*
12.1 Scales and Uses of Indicators   *107*

Foreword

In its pursuit of improved living standards, the world has paid relatively little attention to the negative effects of economic development on the environment. This is especially true in the developing countries. Proof that economic development and the environment are closely interrelated is available everywhere, from major urban settings to the farthest reaches of the tropical forests. The challenge now is to ensure that development strategies for economic growth are implemented in harmony with environmental sustainability. This book touches on a broad range of practical issues related to environmental management, including wealth creation, institutions, equity, energy, trade, human health, and ecological sustainability. The volume is intended for decisionmakers, policy analysts, representatives of nongovernmental organizations, and others interested in understanding and contributing to environmentally sustainable development.

This book was developed as part of a five-year program of policy seminars on economic development and environmental management as well as economic globalization and environmental sustainability. The seminars were held in several regions, including South and East Asia, Eastern Europe, Central Asia, the Black Sea and Caucasus region, southern Africa, Central America, and South America. They were conducted by the World Bank Institute in collaboration with the Foundation for Advanced Studies on International Development, Japan, and with the support of the governments of Japan and the Netherlands. The material benefited from suggestions made by researchers and practitioners from the World Bank and other organizations.

Vinod Thomas
Vice President
World Bank Institute

Acknowledgments

This book is based on presentations in a series of World Bank Institute policy seminars on economic development and environmental management, and later on economic globalization and environmental sustainability. The seminars were initiated in collaboration with the Foundation for Advanced Studies on International Development in Japan and funded by the government of Japan, and later by the government of the Netherlands. Each regional seminar involved a local partner institution. These were the Sabah Foundation, Kota Kinabalu, Malaysia; the Ministry of Environment, Sofia, Bulgaria; the Inter-State Council for the Aral Sea, Tashkent, Uzbekistan; the Black Sea University, Mangalia, Romania; the Southern Africa Development Community, Harare, Zimbabwe; the Central American Commission for Economic Integration Guatemala City, Guatemala; the Central American Commission for Environment and Development San José, Costa Rica; and the South Asian Association for Regional Cooperation, Kathmandu, Nepal.

The editors would like to acknowledge the contributions of the following: Susan Assaf, Tariq Banuri, Robert Clement-Jones, Maria C. J. Cruz, Wilfrido Cruz, Rimma Dankova, Marleen Dijkman, John Dixon, Richard Feachem, Per Fredriksson, Tatuo Fujimura, Frank B. Golley, Kirk Hamilton, Patrice Harou, Clyde Hertzman, Gordon Hughes, Kaori Ishii, Kanta Kumari, Julian Lampietti, Norman Meyers, J. Moyo, K. Muir-Lerresche, Muthukumara S. Mani, Mohan Munasinghe, K. Ramani, Alfredo Sfeir-Younis, R. Paul Shaw, Kazuhiko Takemoto, Vinod Thomas, William Ward, Jeremy Warford, and Manuel Winograd. They are also grateful to the following for their assistance: Fadi Balesh, Sylvia Karlsson, and Rie Tsutsumi.

1

Economic Development and Environmental Sustainability: An Overview

In recent times, most people have viewed economic development as the most important way to reduce poverty and raise living standards. This has led nations to pursue economic growth, and has resulted in impressive economic gains worldwide. However, more than a billion people around the world still live in acute poverty, and the earth's population is likely to double in the next 40 years. This implies that far more economic development will be required to achieve acceptable minimal standards of living for everyone.

Economic Development and the Environment

In this context, two points are vital. First, the world should pursue development while at the same time attempting to eliminate differences between the rich and the poor. In other words, distribution of wealth must remain the top priority. Second, economic development must be achieved in an environmentally sustainable manner. Countries have to find a durable equilibrium between their economy and their ecology. The two areas are closely interrelated, and if they neglect either of them, the chances are that the repercussions will be felt in the other. They should therefore give top priority to reducing pollution and environmental degradation, as well as protecting biodiversity.

Most countries have pursued economic development without taking environmental issues into account. They are now facing the consequences: water and air pollution, pesticides in the food supply, ultraviolet rays penetrating the thinning ozone layer, increased global temperatures caused by greenhouse gases, and so on. The only positive aspect of these problems is that they provide a lesson in terms of mistakes made that should be avoided in the future. Another aspect of the headlong pursuit of economic development that countries must consider is irreversibility, particularly in the context of environmental degradation and loss of biodiversity. Once biodiversity loss has escalated to the point of no return, reversing the situation is impossible. Under such circumstances societies will have to adapt to and cope with environmental changes and hope that the loss of biodiversity will not have too negative an effect on their livelihoods.

Several steps need to be taken to reduce pollution, improve the quality of the ambient environment, and reduce poverty. These steps are the subject of this book. To achieve results, all parties and stakeholders will have to make an effort, and collaboration between governments, civil society, nongovernmental organizations, private industry, and other institutions is essential.

Organization of the Book

Chapter 2

This chapter examines the links between socioeconomic systems and the biophysical environment. As a necessary first step in understanding the problem of environmental degradation and attempting to solve it, it starts by examining more closely the importance of the environment, from which human economies constantly extract numerous benefits, and listing the functions of and services provided by the environment. It then clarifies the concept of sustainable development together with its implications, which inevitably raises questions about intergenerational equity and intragenerational equity.

The chapter also briefly explains the concept of capital to tackle the question of intergenerational equity. Finally, it examines policy recommendations for sustainable development, namely:

- *Correcting the prices.* This section examines the roles of markets and of governments and exposes the reasons behind the existence of market failures.
- *Mainstreaming environmental considerations into economywide policies.* Historically, economists have focused mainly on the project level when dealing with the environment; however, this section explains the importance of adopting a holistic view of the economy. Environmental stewardship is not only a concern for governments, but also for the population at large. Environmental concerns need not only be part of the mandate of a ministry of the environment, but also of all other ministries. Furthermore, other institutions must be proactive as well. At the center of all this infrastructure lies the main actor, the individual.
- *Developing sustainability indicators.* The most important and efficient step in pursuing sustainable development is to change most countries' current national accounting systems. National indexes that show how much nations are growing must reflect the relationship between environmental and socioeconomic systems. For instance, a country could easily burn all its forests and achieve huge increases in its gross domestic product, but its national accounting system is unlikely to show the effect of environmental degradation of natural resources. However, such a country is clearly on an unsustainable path, and in the long run will face huge social, environmental, and economic problems.

Chapter 3

This chapter examines the ecological basis of environmental sustainability. A good understanding of how ecosystems interact will facilitate mainstreaming environmental concerns into policymaking. Environmental sustainability needs to be seen in an evolutionary context; therefore, this chapter examines evolutionary theory. It then looks at the importance of stress and how ecosystems react to it. The regeneration of ecosystems is a function of the level of disturbance, which is often of anthropogenic origin. Finally, the chapter lays the groundwork for policymaking and its interrelationships based on ecological axioms. The main objective of policymaking is to avoid irreversible environmental degeneration, and thus the stage when ecosystems are unable to rehabilitate themselves. With biodiversity loss, humans are facing uncertain outcomes, and by reducing their options are putting themselves in a tenuous position, perhaps even jeopardizing their own survival.

Chapter 4

This chapter examines the dynamics of creating and maintaining wealth. It starts by defining what wealth is and how capital relates to it, and then considers and explains three of the most prominent indicators that monitor how an economy is progressing, namely, the eco-domestic product, wealth accounts, and genuine savings.

Capital may be divided in many parts, and this chapter suggests that one way to divide it is into natural capital, physical capital, financial capital, human resources capital, social (institutional) capital, and philosophical (cultural) capital. It takes a closer look at the importance of social capital, which can also be referred to as institutional resources capital, because this concept relates to the political institutions that shape an economy and set the rules of the game. Finally, the chapter attempts to integrate genuine savings and social capital into policy.

Chapter 5

Having underlined the importance of institutions in dealing with sustainable development, this chapter now goes into this issue in greater detail. Without a well-functioning, formal institutional infrastructure that can support an environmental strategy, good designs will never be translated into reality. Furthermore, knowledge accumulation and dissemination are two critical components of environmental management.

The chapter also stresses the importance of public participation and decentralization. Involving the public in both the design and the implementation of environmental management is critical for two reasons: first, ethically and ideologically people should have the freedom to choose their own direction of development and to influence their means of livelihood. Second, research has shown that projects from which the public has been excluded during the policymaking and implementation phases have frequently failed.

Chapter 6

This chapter addresses the sensitive issue of poverty and income distribution and relates it to environmental management. It explains the classical, mainstream point of view about the links between poverty and the environment, but then presents another interesting point of view.

The mainstream view of the links between poverty and environmental resource degradation is that the planning time horizon of the poor is usually short, and they have few options available to them. As a result, too often they are forced to produce more food by intensifying their use of natural resources, which in turn can drive them deeper into poverty. The alternative view states that thinking in this way implies making three major, unjustified assumptions about the poor, namely: (a) their only or preferred means of sustenance is overextraction of natural resources; (b) their ignorance of both the limitations of their environmental resources and the consequences of their extractive practices; and (c) their small stake in the health and productivity of natural resources. In many cases poor communities have developed ways to sustain themselves based on the limitations and potential of their local natural resource base, and in some instances, traditional knowledge has actually improved the health of local ecosystems.

Chapter 7

This chapter examines trends in population growth and their relationship to natural resource degradation. Projections indicate that by 2025 the world's population will total about 8.3 billion people (compared with nearly 6 billion now), with the bulk of growth in developing countries. Obviously, this is likely to place even more pressure on natural resources, because of increased consumption. Related problems are likely to include worse water, soil, and air pollution; greater waste generation; further loss of biodiversity; and higher rates of deforestation and desertification. This implies that a comprehensive population policy is important for a long-term solution to environmental problems.

The chapter then looks at some policy recommendations, such as (a) improving literacy rates; (b) empowering women as managers in decisions concerning the environment and family planning; (c) acquiring better information for decisionmaking and collecting data about those aspects of demographic trends that have the greatest impacts on the environment; (d) encouraging the involvement of the public and of nongovernmental organizations in environmental issues; and (e) reviewing family planning efforts in the context of macroeconomic and sectoral policies, particularly education and health. While countries need to find ways to decrease the rate of population growth, at the same time they should try to maximize the few positive effects that such growth engenders.

Chapter 8

Environmental issues cannot be discussed without addressing one of the main causes of pollution, energy production. Heavy dependence on fossil fuels is resulting in the emission of large amounts of greenhouse gases. Power plants are responsible not only for contributing to global air pollution and to the greenhouse effect, but also for having serious detrimental effects on local populations and ecosystems. In some developing countries, local air pollution is the most urgent problem.

Other sources of energy are also causing pollution or degradation of the environment, for instance, hydroelectric power is responsible for flooding large areas, destroying ecosystems, and displacing people, and nuclear power generates radioactive waste that is unsafe and hard to dispose of.

The policy response to these issues can be divided into four major components aimed at securing a sustainable energy supply in the long run: (a) increasing energy efficiency, (b) reducing negative environmental impacts through technological advances, (c) using alternative energy sources, and (d) implementing policy reforms.

Chapter 9

This chapter examines the complex links between trade and the environment. Trade among countries has extremely important effects on economic growth and environmental quality; however, the net effect of trade on the environment is still unclear. The major effect of trade is its tendency to increase economic activity, which in turn motivates economywide changes that have environmental impacts. These impacts may be negative or positive, depending on the country's environmental strategy. If policies are environmentally sound, institutional infrastructure is effective, property rights are well established, and market failures are minimized, then trade-induced economic growth could result in some positive environmental effects, and thereby in some positive welfare gains.

This chapter addresses the issue of environmental regulations and competitiveness. Little empirical evidence supports the argument that competitiveness and trade would suffer from environmental policy. Industries have relocated because of a variety of other reasons than environmental policy, such as market factors, worker safety regulations, and mandatory relocation as in the case of hazardous chemical manufacturers. Other adaptations are generally more cost-effective than relocation. By contrast, ecolabeling could affect trade and induce positive environmental impacts. By isolating those countries or companies that are not producing environmentally friendly products, ecolabeling may act as a trade barrier.

Chapter 10

This chapter is devoted to global environmental issues and looks at environmental problems in a more holistic fashion. Global environmental problems are extremely complex and include the greenhouse effect, the destruction of the ozone layer, and the loss of biodiversity. One reason for their complexity is that countries are reluctant to address these issues, because the costs to a given country are far greater than the benefits. Moreover, by definition, global environmental problems transcend administrative jurisdictions and national borders. Finally, there is a pronounced lack of information about the effects of such global environmental problems.

International collaboration is the key for resolving these issues. One example given in the chapter is the Aral Sea Program, where despite their differences and political divergences, countries have come together to address the problems facing the Aral Sea. International institutions and conventions are needed to provide an infrastructure that permits and protects such collaboration. The chapter discusses six major conventions, namely: the Montreal Protocol, the Framework Convention for Climate Change, the Basel Convention, the Convention on Combating Desertification, the Convention on Biological Diversity, and the Convention on International Trade in Endangered Species. Finally, the chapter examines the creation of a carbon market.

Chapter 11

Clearly, the most important reason why the world as a whole is now taking environmental degradation more seriously than in the past is because of the anthropocentric way of human thinking. Only now are people realizing how unsustainable use of natural resources is having so many detrimental effects on their own health and survival, and consequently starting to worry and to take action.

Estimates indicate that poor environmental quality is currently directly responsible for some 25 percent of all preventable ill-health, with diarrheal diseases and respiratory infections heading the list. The environments in which humans live can be divided into three categories: the household environment, the occupational environment, and the ambient environment. The chapter examines each of these separately in terms of the risks that may be present within each.

Finally, the chapter looks at the techniques that attempt to place a value on mortality, namely, the willingness to pay, the wage differential, and the human capital approaches, and on morbidity using either the cost of illness or the preventive expenditures techniques.

Chapter 12

The book concludes by looking at planning and environmental indicators and underlining the importance of information and knowledge. As concerns the environment and sustainable development, decisionmakers have faced many difficulties because of the lack of information, the inaccessibility of data, or the poor quality of information, or because of standardization problems. Hence this chapter discusses the challenges of assembling, analyzing, and simplifying data for measuring sustainable development.

Indicators are summarized or aggregated data are selected and transformed from primary data sets. Levels of aggregation go from primary data, to analyzed data, to simple indicators, and finally to indexes. The criteria for indicator selection are (a) policy relevance and utility to users, (b) analytical soundness, and (c) measurability. Improved indicators of environmental sustainability enhance decisionmaking at all levels and increase awareness among the public, which in turn results in more effective and creative problem solving.

2

Policy Implications for Sustainable Development

Policymakers often emphasize economic growth as the most important way to reduce poverty, raise living standards, and manage the environment. This justifies the increased consumption of natural resources for generating economic activity. At the same time, policymakers have shown less concern about the rate of resource depletion or the effects of waste products on socioeconomic systems and on the environment itself.

Human Society and the Environment

When economists developed modern economic theories in parallel with emerging industrialization processes, they viewed the socioeconomic system as separate from and independent of the natural environment. They considered natural resources to be free goods available for extraction, and societies returned waste to the environment without cost or further consideration. Views have changed since those times, and traditional wisdom embodied in major religious systems and recent scientific evidence underlines that economic development depends directly on environmental quality and the goods and services provided by the environment.

The model of how socioeconomic systems connect to the environment has changed substantially in recent times (figure 2.1), and the socioeconomic system—composed of various forms of capital—is very much part of our environment. Society uses, and is heavily dependent on, the environment as the "source"

Figure 2.1. *The Relationship between the Socioeconomic System and the Environment*

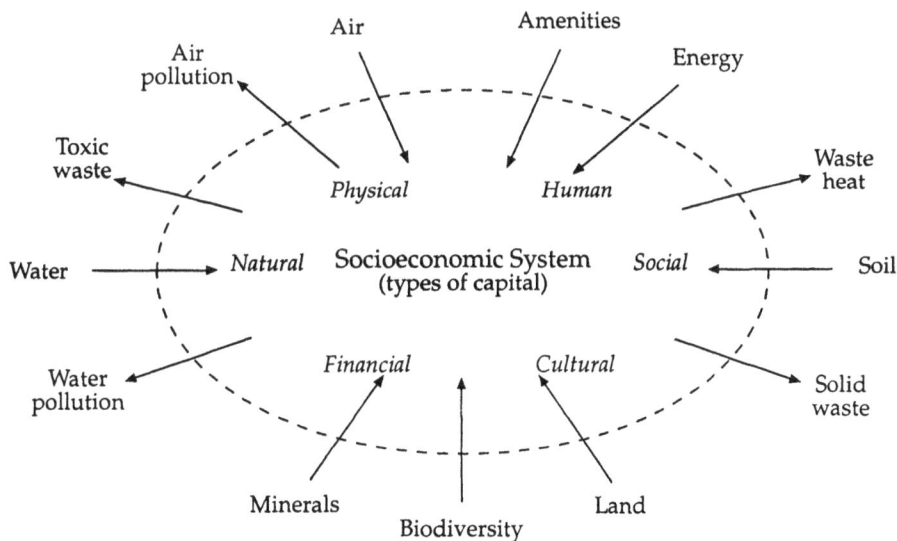

Source: Authors.

Based on presentations by Tariq Banuri, José Furtado, Mohan Munasinghe, Bill Ward, and Alfredo Sfeir Younis.

of a range of services and resources. At the same time, society uses (or abuses) and depends heavily on the environment as a "sink" or repository for its pollution and waste. The source and sink services are in scarce supply and are continually being degraded and limited by economic activities.

Linked to the source and sink functions, ecologists have identified four main functions that the environment provides, all of which are inextricably linked to ecological processes (table 2.1):

- *Regulation functions.* The environment sustains life-support systems, such as tropical forests, oceans, mangrove swamps, and coral reefs.
- *Production functions.* The environment's inputs are a direct contribution to economic activity (oil, coal, fuelwood, minerals).
- *Carrier functions.* The environment and natural resources such as clean air and clean water contribute to the quality of life, for example, they contribute to physical health.
- *Information functions.* The environment is valued as an amenity with intrinsic worth, for instance, people appreciate natural landscapes and enjoy them through recreational activities.

All these ecological functions are important for maintaining the overall performance and integrity of ecosystems and are fundamental for sustaining life (see chapter 3). Given the pressures on these systems from economic activity and population growth, a new, integrated approach for development is needed.

Sustainable Development

An approach to development that has been the subject of much debate and consensus building during the last two decades of the 20th century is known as sustainable development. The most commonly cited definition of this concept is from the World Commission on Environment and Development (1987, p. 43). In this report the commission launched the concept and defined it as being development that "meets the needs of the present generation without compromising the ability of future generations to meet their own needs."

Table 2.1. Functions and Services Provided by the Environment

Regulation functions	Production functions	Carrier functions	Information functions
Providing support for economic activity and human welfare through • Protection against harmful cosmic influences • Climate regulation • Watershed protection and catchment • Erosion prevention and soil protection • Storage and recycling of industrial and human waste • Maintenance of biological and genetic diversity • Biological control • Provisions of migratory, nursery, and feeding habitats	Providing basic resources such as • Oxygen • Food and drinking water • Water for industrial use, households, and so forth • Materials for making clothing and fabrics • Building, construction, and manufacturing materials • Energy and fuels • Minerals • Medicinal, bio-chemical, genetic, and ornamental resources	Providing space and a suitable substrate for, among other things, • Habitation • Agriculture, forestry, fisheries, aquaculture • Industry • Engineering projects, such as dams and roads • Recreation • Nature conservation	Providing aesthetic, cultural, and scientific benefits through • Aesthetic information • Spiritual and religious information • Cultural and artistic inspiration • Educational and scientific information • Potential information

Source: Heywood (1995, p. 879).

This definition of sustainable development is an intuitively appealing concept, but is not easily translated into practice, because sustainability can hold different meanings for different groups of people and can take different forms. At the international level, the United Nations Conference on Environment and Development, known as the Earth Summit, held in Rio de Janeiro in 1992, endorsed the goal of sustainable development in the Rio Declaration (appendix 1). Agenda 21, intended to achieve this goal, is an action plan for the 21st century (appendix 2). Both these documents outline the concept and establish actions that foster sustainable development. The concept of sustainable development thus emerged as a desirable goal for society.

The World Commission on Environment and Development's definition of sustainable development raises several issues, namely:

- How do intermediate and long-run decisions on resource management affect equity between people of different generations (intergenerational equity) and equity between people of the same generation (intragenerational equity)?
- What should we leave to future generations to ensure that they are not disadvantaged by present consumption:
  - The same physical stock of resources, or
  - The same amount of resources per capita, or
  - The potential for being at least as well off in an economic and social sense?
- What are the policy implications of sustainable development?

Intergenerational Equity

The question of intergenerational equity is at the core of the definition of sustainability, and prompts debate on what societies value and how to transfer these values to future generations. Paths viewed as economically optimal for development today may not be sustainable for future generations (figure 2.2). If welfare considerations are taken into account, economically optimal paths may not be sustainable in the long run. Moreover, sustainable paths may not necessarily be economically optimal.

The challenge is to achieve a balanced approach to development in terms of optimality (see figure 2.2 for a definition) and sustainability. One way to do this is to hold capital stocks constant from generation to generation. Capital consists of several types:

- Man-made or physical capital (K_m)—machines, factories, and roads
- Human capital (K_h)—the stock of knowledge, skills, and health
- Natural capital (K_n)—the stock of natural assets or environmental assets, for example, soil fertility, forests, fisheries, biodiversity, waste assimilation capacity, oil, gas, coal, the ozone layer, biogeochemical cycles
- Financial capital (K_f)—equity and debt that represent claims on physical or working assets
- Social capital (K_i)—formal and informal institutions that consist of laws, economic policies, property rights, and codes of conduct
- Cultural and spiritual capital (K_c)—behavioral influences, sometimes defined as informal institutions, that affect human decisions and actions (while this type of capital is particularly difficult to identify, it has a significant impact on how people make decisions).

We can therefore look upon the total stock of capital, K, as

$$K = K_m + K_h + K_n + K_f + K_i + K_c + K^*$$

where K^* denotes capital of a critical nature for which a substitute is difficult or impossible to find.

Some types of capital can be substituted for other types, such as coal for oil. Other types of capital may be more difficult, or even impossible, to substitute, such as the ozone layer. Whether or not capital is substitutable helps in ascribing a market value to it; however, the problem here is that markets do not exist for some types of capital. This is especially true in the case of many of the environmental functions and services mentioned earlier (table 2.1). Moreover, because our knowledge about ecosystems and their complex interactions is incomplete (see chapter 3), the relative importance of particular functions is difficult to ascertain.

To preserve intergenerational equity, the total amount of capital that is passed on to the next generation should not be less than the capital the current generation inherited. The proportion of the different kinds of capital that is passed on may vary, but capital that is passed on should include capital that cannot be substituted. This ensures the transfer of an overall equivalent level of welfare to the next generation. The major constraints in applying this concept of capital are (a) that no single method is available for measuring the different forms of capital to gain some insight into their equivalence, and hence their substitutability, and (b) that different forms of capital are associated with different behavior patterns in relation to their use.

Intragenerational Equity

Improved environmental quality is likely to help achieve intragenerational equity. Currently, affluent sections of the population can protect themselves against environmental damage more easily because

Figure 2.2. *Optimality, Sustainability, and Survivability of Development*

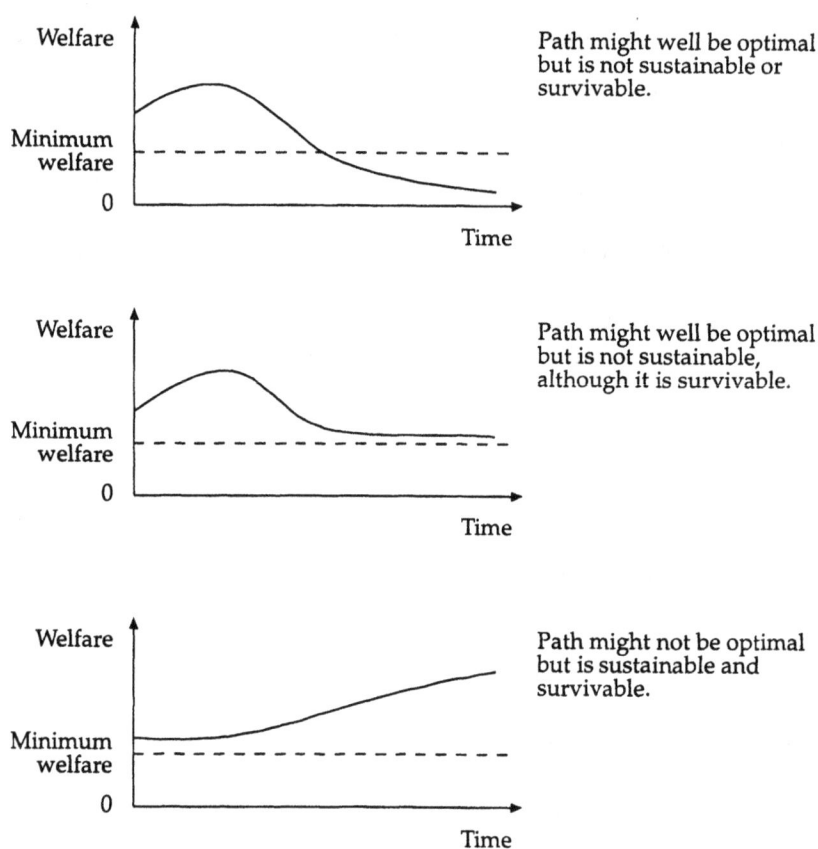

Note: Optimality is a path of development that maximizes the present values of future gains in human welfare. Sustainability is human welfare that rises, or at least does not fall, over time. Survivability is a path of development that lies above a minimum level of welfare. Anything below it is not survivable. Being fair to the future could be interpreted as ensuring that the welfare path never falls over time.

Source: Pearce and Warford (1993, p. 50).

they have more resources than the impoverished, for instance, wealthy urban elites can protect themselves against contaminated water by buying bottled water. This also applies to the agriculture sector, as some evidence indicates that the prospects for people's future livelihood may decrease as environments become degraded. For example, as cut and burn techniques become pervasive, land quality and water availability diminish, thus environmental degradation may exacerbate poverty, which will further intensify pressures on the environment through increased land degradation, thereby reinforcing this cycle (see chapter 6).

Policy Recommendations for Sustainable Development

This section briefly discusses three broad economic policy recommendations for sustainable development (subsequent chapters go into these recommendations in greater detail), namely:

- Correcting prices, which is the responsibility of markets and governments
- Mainstreaming environmental considerations into economywide policies, sector work, and cost-benefit analysis of projects
- Devising sustainability indicators in an attempt to modify systems of national accounts.

Correcting Prices

Markets frequently do not reflect the social cost of the environment accurately for several reasons. Above all, this is because the environment is a public good. Public goods are characterized by low exclusion and nonrivalry. Low exclusion means that the good will be supplied to all groups and all groups can benefit from the good, because no one group can be excluded. Thus if air quality is improved because of the efforts of a particular group, people who did not exert any effort to improve air quality can still enjoy its benefits. Nonrivalry means that one person's use of the resource does not reduce its availability to others. For example, one person's consumption of air does not affect someone else's potential for air consumption.

Goods with low exclusion and nonrivalry are difficult to exchange in the market. Because no natural markets exist for such goods, they can easily be consumed and abused. In the case of air quality, the prices of polluting products do not reflect their adverse effects on the public in terms of health, aesthetic value, and so forth. Thus polluters do not take the cost of air pollution into consideration, and such effects are called externalities. The result is excessive air pollution.

The following are some of the reasons for market failure:

- *Lack of markets.* Many vital environmental services are not traded in the market. For example, in the case of tropical rain forests, timber is marketed, but watershed protection is not. The nonmarketed benefits are frequently ignored, and the benefits of the resource are overexploited.
- *Lack of property rights.* Unclear or nonexistent property rights result in overexploitation, because no one is responsible for the resource. A "mining" mentality as concerns resource use occurs because long-term responsibility or liability does not exist. For instance, overfishing often occurs because of the lack of individual water rights. This leads to declines in fish stocks and diminishing levels of biodiversity (gene, species, and ecosystem diversity).
- *Lack of information.* Individuals and societies lack information about environmental impacts or about low-cost ways to avoid damage. In the case of chlorofluorocarbons and ozone depletion, private firms may not be aware of technologies that will give them the same financial benefits, but limit environmental harm. Moreover, at the individual level, increased information about the environment can have a huge impact on the way societies view, use, and conserve the environment. Another aspect of information asymmetry is a lack of transparency about environmental policy and about private sector decisions in relation to natural resource use and environmental damage.

In addition to market failure, another countervailing force on environmental quality is policy failure. Occasionally, economic policy can result in inefficient outcomes. For example, inefficient interventions may include subsidies, price controls, exchange controls, and ownership controls. A common example of policy failure is keeping prices below market prices. This generates inefficiency and can lead to excessive or wasteful use of natural resources. Institutional failure or weakness can also adversely affect natural resource management.

Mainstreaming Environmental Considerations

Environmental and natural resource issues can be crucial to the success or failure of development projects, programs, or policies. In recent years, the trend has been to analyze the impact of overall macroeconomic policies on the environment, in addition to evaluating sector- and project-specific impacts on the environment. Evaluating environmental impacts has become an important part of cost-benefit analysis, along with the traditional objectives of economic efficiency, equity, and financial and administrative feasibility.

The impacts of economic activities on the environment can be divided into three broad categories as follows:

- Physical impacts, for example, loss of fertile topsoil, waste discharge into water
- Biological impacts, for example, loss of plant and animal species
- Sociological impacts, for example, displacement of local people from a dam construction site and/ or cultural erosion.

Incorporating environmental considerations into cost-benefit analyses essentially involves identifying impacts and imputing a value to them. Sustainability considerations are addressed when the project includes ways to deal with its negative environmental impacts. Although these developments are important, the integration of environmental considerations into development planning is needed on a much broader level. Mainstreaming environmental considerations means that environmental stewardship is not only a concern for governments, but that societies also share the values underlying all aspects of environmental goods and services. Mainstreaming requires substantive, and sometimes radical, reforms, not only in administrative structures, but also in institutional and human behavior. At a minimum, it requires increased education and information about the environment so as to make the environment a central focus of decisionmaking across all levels of government, private sector activities, communities, and individuals. Society as a whole must see these changes as a dynamic and fluid process that evolves to suit the particular situation or problem at hand.

Figure 2.3 shows some examples of actors and actions that can be involved in mainstreaming environmental considerations. At the center are individuals, who need to change their values in a way that shows more concern for their fellow human beings and other parts of the ecosystem. Individuals' values can then be translated into action at all levels of society: local, national, and global.

Devising Sustainability Indicators

A third area where policy change is needed is accounting systems. Countries need to create more accurate national accounting systems that reflect the relationship between the environment and socioeconomic systems more closely (figure 2.1). The current system—the gross national product—measures the aggregate value of the output of a country's economy in a given year and does not record deterioration of the environment, which may negatively affect economic welfare.

Ecological systems are far too complex to place a value on them or to design an accurate indicator of their state of well-being. Nonetheless, current national account systems need to be modified so that some environmental values are gradually recognized and can be compared across countries. Later chapters discuss pertinent issues in detail; however, to summarize, shortcomings of current accounting systems include the following:

Figure 2.3. Mainstreaming Environmental Considerations: Examples of Actors and Actions

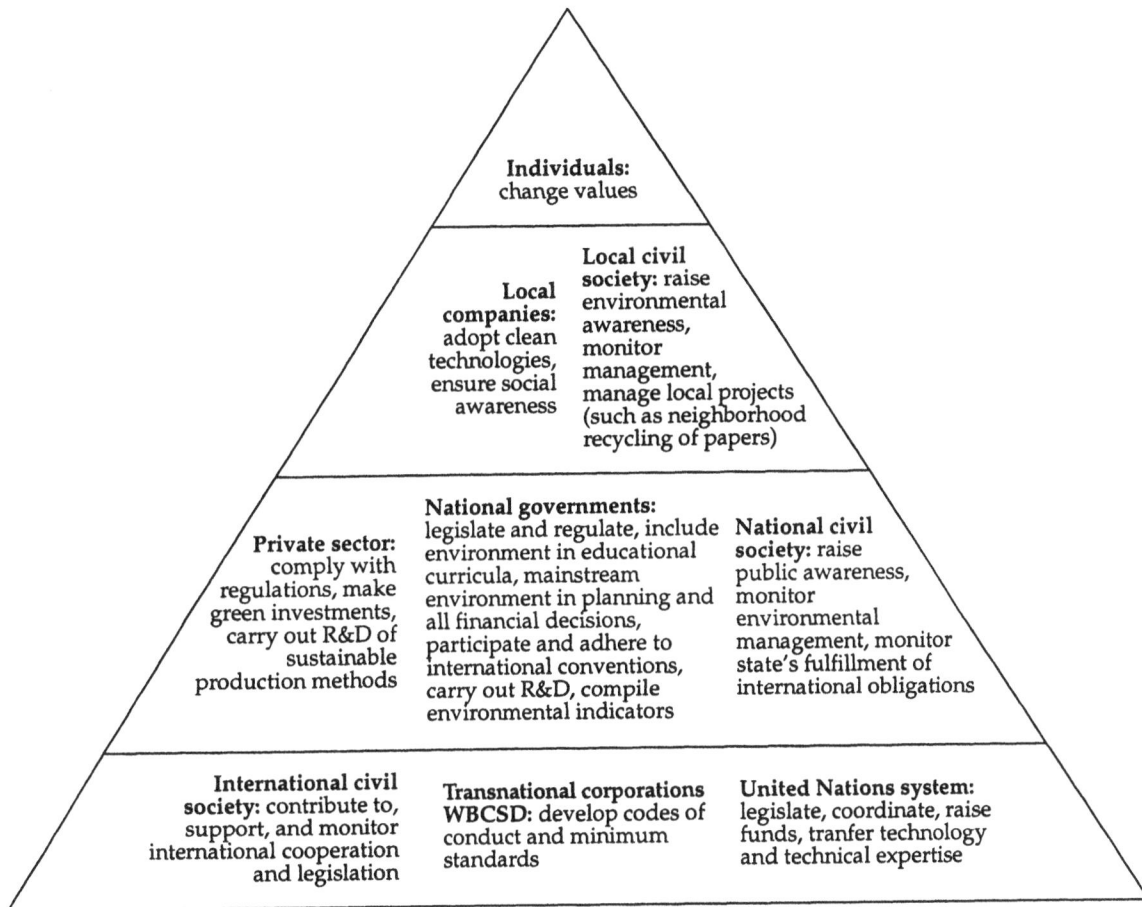

R&D Research and development.
WBCSD World Business Council for Sustainable Development.
Source: Authors.

- They make assumptions about what is important now and what will be important in the future.
- They are unable to account for irreversibilities, such as species loss, or characteristics that cannot be represented in monetary terms.
- They often do a poor job of taking uncertainty into account.
- They emphasize flow variables and do not account for stocks of natural resources.
- They emphasize quantities that enter into commerce.
- They are based on linear relationships that cannot be reconciled with ecological functions.

Some of the assumptions should be modified so that stocks of natural capital are viewed as an asset and environmental deterioration as a liability. Thus, for example, the stock of natural capital would decrease when resources such as oil reserves or standing forests were depleted. However, modifying accounting systems can be both complex and costly. A feasible first step could be to publish a separate set of accounts that showed current resource use in nonmonetary units as is done in France and Norway. Table 2.2 shows the physical accounts for forest resources in France and is an example of the assignment of a value to some of the functions of natural systems. Such accounts are designed to aid planning and decisionmaking. They help trace the environmental effects of policy changes and of general trends in

Table 2.2.   *Physical Account for Commercial Forests in France, 1969–79*
(thousands of cubic meters)

Resource or use	Broadleaf	Coniferous	Total
Resource (asset)			
Volume of growing stock in 1969	980.1	6,526.5	7,506.6
Natural growth of initial stock	401.0	2,583.5	2,984.5
Natural growth by reproduction	41.1	258.4	299.5
Total	1,422.2	9,368.4	10,790.6
Use			
Natural reduction (mortality)	5.6	21.0	26.6
Accidental reduction (breakage and windfall)	9.7	481.2	490.9
Resource extraction (commercial felling)	97.0	1,474.0	1,566.0
Self-consumption	13.6	395.0	408.6
Adjustment	-29.4	+1,239.2	1,209.8
Volume of growing stock in 1979	1,330.7	5,758.4	7,088.7
Total	1,422.2	9,368.4	10,790.6

Source: Pearce and Warford (1993, p. 92).

the economy and add an environmental dimension to the economic planning process. A number of methods that can measure various values of the numerous functions of ecosystems are available. Once such values are integrated into national accounts, then such accounts would more closely reflect the goals of sustainable development.

Conclusion

The goal of achieving development that is sustainable and does not threaten the livelihoods and well-being of future generations has been almost universally endorsed. While placing a value on the different kinds of capital that a society is built upon (physical, human, natural, financial, social, cultural, and spiritual) is not possible, their importance for sustainable development is nonetheless substantial, and future generations will benefit from current consideration of the development and substitutability of each component.

One fundamental condition for achieving the goal of sustainable development is to realize that environmental quality and the general services performed by the natural environment play a more important role than development planners and economic managers had assumed in the past. The broad policy implications of sustainable development suggest that countries should focus on the role of the government and the market to compensate for environmental externalities, should mainstream environmental considerations into program and project planning, and should modify their national accounts to include environmental services.

Appendix 1. Rio Declaration on Environment and Development

The United Nations Conference on Environment and Development,
Having met at Rio de Janeiro from 3 to 14 June 1992,
Reaffirming the Declaration of the United Nations Conference on the Human Environment, adopted at Stockholm on 16 June 1972, and seeking to build upon it,
With the goal of establishing a new and equitable global partnership through the creation of new levels of cooperation among States, key sectors of societies and people,
Working towards international agreements which respect the interests of all and protect the integrity of the global environmental and developmental system,

Recognizing the integral and interdependent nature of the Earth, our home,
Proclaims that:

Principle 1

Human beings are at the centre of concerns for sustainable development. They are entitled to a healthy and productive life in harmony with nature.

Principle 2

States have, in accordance with the Charter of the United Nations and the principles of international law, the sovereign right to exploit their own resources pursuant to their own environmental and developmental policies, and the responsibility to ensure that activities within their jurisdiction or control do not cause damage to the environment of other States or of areas beyond the limits of national jurisdiction.

Principle 3

The right to development must be fulfilled so as to equitably meet developmental and environmental needs of present and future generations.

Principle 4

In order to achieve sustainable development, environmental protection shall constitute an integral part of the development process and cannot be considered in isolation from it.

Principle 5

All States and all people shall cooperate in the essential task of eradicating poverty as an indispensable requirement for sustainable development, in order to decrease the disparities in standards of living and better meet the needs of the majority of the people of the world.

Principle 6

The special situation and needs of developing countries, particularly the least developed and those most environmentally vulnerable, shall be given special priority. International actions in the field of environment and development should also address the interests and needs of all countries.

Principle 7

States shall cooperate in a spirit of global partnership to conserve, protect and restore the health and integrity of the Earth's ecosystem. In view of the different contributions to global environmental degradation, States have common but differentiated responsibilities. The developed countries acknowledge the responsibility that they bear in the international pursuit of sustainable development in view of the pressures their societies place on the global environment and of the technologies and financial resources they command.

Principle 8

To achieve sustainable development and a higher quality of life for all people, States should reduce and eliminate unsustainable patterns of production and consumption and promote appropriate demographic policies.

Principle 9

States should cooperate to strengthen endogenous capacity-building for sustainable development by improving scientific understanding through exchanges of scientific and technological knowledge, and by enhancing the development, adaptation, diffusion and transfer of technologies, including new and innovative technologies.

Principle 10

Environmental issues are best handled with the participation of all concerned citizens, at the relevant level. At the national level, each individual shall have appropriate access to information concerning the environment that is held by public authorities, including information on hazardous materials and activities in their communities, and the opportunity to participate in decision-making processes. States shall facilitate and encourage public awareness and participation by making information widely available. Effective access to judicial and administrative proceedings, including redress and remedy, shall be provided.

Principle 11

States shall enact effective environmental legislation. Environmental standards, management objectives and priorities should reflect the environmental and developmental context to which they apply. Standards applied by some countries may be inappropriate and of unwarranted economic and social cost to other countries, in particular developing countries.

Principle 12

States should cooperate to promote a supportive and open international economic system that would lead to economic growth and sustainable development in all countries, to better address the problems of environmental degradation. Trade policy measures for environmental purposes should not constitute a means of arbitrary or unjustifiable discrimination or a disguised restriction on international trade. Unilateral actions to deal with environmental challenges outside the jurisdiction of the importing country should be avoided. Environmental measures addressing transboundary or global environmental problems should, as far as possible, be based on an international consensus.

Principle 13

States shall develop national law regarding liability and compensation for the victims of pollution and other environmental damage. States shall also cooperate in an expeditious and more determined manner to develop further international law regarding liability and compensation for adverse effects of environmental damage caused by activities within their jurisdiction or control to areas beyond their jurisdiction.

Principle 14

States should effectively cooperate to discourage or prevent the relocation and transfer to other States of any activities and substances that cause severe environmental degradation or are found to be harmful to human health.   .

Principle 15

In order to protect the environment, the precautionary approach shall be widely applied by States according to their capabilities. Where there are threats of serious or irreversible damage, lack of full scientific certainty shall not be used as a reason for postponing cost-effective measures to prevent environmental degradation.

Principle 16

National authorities should endeavour to promote the internalization of environmental costs and the use of economic instruments, taking into account the approach that the polluter should, in principle, bear the cost of pollution, with due regard to the public interest and without distorting international trade and investment.

Principle 17

Environmental impact assessment, as a national instrument, shall be undertaken for proposed activities that are likely to have a significant adverse impact on the environment and are subject to a decision of a competent national authority.

Principle 18

States shall immediately notify other States of any natural disasters or other emergencies that are likely to produce sudden harmful effects on the environment of those States. Every effort shall be made by the international community to help States so afflicted.

Principle 19

States shall provide prior and timely notification and relevant information to potentially affected States on activities that may have a significant adverse transboundary environmental effect and shall consult with those States at an early stage and in good faith.

Principle 20

Women have a vital role in environmental management and development. Their full participation is therefore essential to achieve sustainable development.

Principle 21

The creativity, ideals and courage of the youth of the world should be mobilized to forge a global partnership in order to achieve sustainable development and ensure a better future for all.

Principle 22

Indigenous people and their communities and other local communities have a vital role in environmental management and development because of their knowledge and traditional practices. States should recognize and duly support their identity, culture and interests and enable their effective participation in the achievement of sustainable development.

Principle 23

The environment and natural resources of people under oppression, domination and occupation shall be protected.

Principle 24

Warfare is inherently destructive of sustainable development. States shall therefore respect international law providing protection for the environment in times of armed conflict and cooperate in its further development, as necessary.

Principle 25

Peace, development and environmental protection are interdependent and indivisible.

Principle 26

States shall resolve all their environmental disputes peacefully and by appropriate means in accordance with the Charter of the United Nations.

Principle 27

States and people shall cooperate in good faith and in a spirit of partnership in the fulfillment of the principles embodied in this Declaration and in the further development of international law in the field of sustainable development.

Appendix 2. Agenda 21, Chapter 1

Preamble

1.1   Humanity stands at a defining moment in history. We are confronted with a perpetuation of disparities between and within nations, a worsening of poverty, hunger, ill health and illiteracy, and the continuing deterioration of the ecosystems on which we depend for our well-being. However, integration of environment and development concerns and greater attention to them will lead to the fulfillment of basic needs, improved living standards for all, better protected and managed ecosystems and a safer, more prosperous future. No nation can achieve this on its own; but together we can—in a global partnership for sustainable development.

1.2   This global partnership must build on the premises of General Assembly resolution 44/228 of 22 December 1989, which was adopted when the nations of the world called for the United Nations Conference on Environment and Development, and on the acceptance of the need to take a balanced and integrated approach to environment and development questions.

1.3   Agenda 21 addresses the pressing problems of today and also aims at preparing the world for the challenges of the next century. It reflects a global consensus and political commitment at the highest level on development and environment cooperation. Its successful implementation is first and foremost the responsibility of Governments. National strategies, plans, policies and processes are crucial in achieving this. International cooperation should support and supplement such national efforts. In this context, the United Nations system has a key role to play. Other international, regional and subregional organizations are also called upon to contribute to this effort. The broadest public participation and the active involvement of the non-governmental organizations and other groups should also be encouraged.

1.4   The developmental and environmental objectives of Agenda 21 will require a substantial flow of new and additional financial resources to developing countries, in order to cover the incremental costs for the actions they have to undertake to deal with global environmental problems and to accelerate sustainable development. Financial resources are also required for strengthening the capacity of international institutions for the implementation of Agenda 21. An indicative order-of-magnitude assessment of costs is included in each of the programme areas. This assessment will need to be examined and refined by the relevant implementing agencies and organizations.

1.5   In the implementation of the relevant programme areas identified in Agenda 21, special attention should be given to the particular circumstances facing the economies in transition. It must also be recognized that these countries are facing unprecedented challenges in transforming their economies, in some cases in the midst of considerable social and political tension.

1.6   The programme areas that constitute Agenda 21 are described in terms of the basis for action, objectives, activities and means of implementation. Agenda 21 is a dynamic programme. It will be carried out by the various actors according to the different situations, capacities and priorities of countries and regions in full respect of all the principles contained in the Rio Declaration on Environment and Development. It could evolve over time in the light of changing needs and circumstances. This process marks the beginning of a new global partnership for sustainable development.

References

Heywood, V. H., ed. 1995. *Global Biodiversity Assessment.* Cambridge, U.K.: Cambridge University Press.

Pearce, David W., and Jeremy J. Warford. 1993. *World Without End.* New York: Oxford University Press.

United Nations Conference on Environment and Development. 1992. *Agenda 21.* New York: United Nations Publications.

World Commission on Environment and Development. 1987. *Our Common Future.* New York: Oxford University Press.

Other Recommended Readings

Dixon, John A., and Louise A. Fallon. 1989. "The Concept of Sustainability: Origins, Extensions, and Usefulness for Policy." *Society and Natural Resources* 2 (2): 73–84.

Goodland, Robert, Herman Daly, and Salah El Sarafy, eds. 1991. *Environmentally Sustainable Economic Development: Building on Brundtland.* New York: United Nations Educational, Scientific, and Cultural Organization.

Munasinghe, Mohan. 1992. *Environmental Economics and Sustainable Development.* Washington, D.C.: World Bank.

Repetto, Robert. 1992. "Key Elements of Sustainable Development." Background paper for the *World Development Report 1992.* World Bank, Washington, D.C.

World Bank. 1992. *World Development Report 1992.* New York: Oxford University Press.

World Resources Institute. 1992. *World Resources 1992–93.* New York: Oxford University Press.

3

Ecological Basis of Environmental Sustainability

The sustainable management of ecosystems and the environmental goods and services they provide follow six fundamental ecological axioms:

- Ecosystem evolution is a continuous, adaptive process.
- Ecological processes are self-organizing, and external energy flow leads to complex ecosystems.
- Ecological processes unfold in systems within systems, and this hierarchical organization differs both in space and time.
- Ecosystems vary in their absorption and regeneration capacity relative to human disturbance.
- Ecosystems comprise the sum of ecological processes, which exceeds the sum of objects or species and materials.
- All ecological processes are interrelated.

A broad understanding of these fundamental characteristics of ecosystems by policymakers, decisionmakers, and civil society should facilitate the mainstreaming of environmental concerns in an ecologically appropriate manner for sustainable development. Ecological processes, by their very nature, place some fundamental limits on human activities. If humans exceed these limits, ecosystems become unstable, and society will ultimately reap the consequences.

Sustainability from the Ecological Perspective

Environmental sustainability needs to be seen in the context of the evolution of life on Earth.

Ecosystem Evolution Is a Continuous, Adaptive Process

The Earth's biosphere formed during the period of planetary cooling some 4 billion years ago. Life forms initially evolved in an environment of considerable physical turbulence in shallow oceans with abundant external energy and mineral resources as complex molecules able to replicate themselves. These life forms first evolved in an anaerobic or deoxygenated aquatic environment, and only about 2 billion years later started evolving in an aerobic or oxygenated environment (table 3.1).

During the anaerobic phase, primitive bacteria and microorganisms took advantage of the Earth's thermal energy, water, and minerals to grow, replicate, and diversify, and released gaseous by-products, such as methane and carbon dioxide. These fermentation by-products helped form the ozone layer through their interaction with radiation, thereby enabling the evolution of life forms protected from ultraviolet radiation. These microorganisms form the basis of the decomposer system or food chain, and while most species are chemo-synthesizers, some species are predators. Microbial species far outnumber known plant and animal species, with each adapted to perform a specific, narrow function.

Diversification of species occurs in tension fields (that is, under conditions of intense competition and natural selection pressures), first through changes in reproductive systems and/or competition for the efficient use of scarce resources (energy, matter, space, time, and information) by a genetically variable population, and second through the dynamics of isolation (by internal or external barriers)

Based on presentations by José Furtado.

21

Table 3.1. Evolution of the Biosphere and Climate

Life stages	Years ago (billions)	Evolutionary stages
Prebiotic	**4.5**	Earth formation
		Cooling of molten lava
	4.0	Oldest rocks; steam condensation
	3.8	Shallow oceans; carbon-based compounds
		Catalytic loops; membranes
Microbiotic	**3.5**	Bacterial cells; anaerobes dominant
Microorganisms		Fermentation; reducing atmosphere
		Primary production very low
		Chemo-photosynthesis
		sensing devices; motion
		DNA repair; gene trading
	2.8	Tectonic plates; continent formation
		Oxygen photosynthesis
	2.5	Bacterial explosive radiation
	2.2	Nucleated cells
	2.0	Photosynthetic autotroph explosive radiation
		Primary production increasing
		Oxygen-forming atmosphere
	1.8	Oxygen breathing
	1.5	Earth surface and atmosphere established
Macrobiotic	1.2	Locomotion
	1.0	Sexual reproduction
	0.8	Mitochondria; chloroplasts
		Blue-green and green algae
Precambrian	0.7	Early animals
Cambrian	0.6	Invertebrates explosive radiation
		Shells and skeletons
Ordovician/Silurian	0.5	Early plants; high primary production
Devonian	0.4	Land vegetation and animals (vertebrates)
		Fossil fuel formation
Permian	0.3	Dinosaurs; Primary production low
Triassic/Jurassic	0.2	Mammals; homeotherms
		Higher plant and animal explosive radiation
Cretaceous	0.1	Flowering plants; primates
		Primary production increasing
Tertiary	0.1– present	Calcareous and siliceous diatoms
		Human evolution and radiation
		Primary production oscillating

and/or natural selection (by physical or biotic factors such as parasites and predators) between populations or different trophic levels. Such diversification occurs within a relatively stable environment that, when saturated by interacting species, moves through an unstable, bounded transition to another stable environmental phase. Thus no two species use an identical combination of resources or perform exactly the same functions in an ecosystem. In using environmental resources and generating wastes, each individual and species changes the nature of the environment for other individuals and species.

As some microorganisms developed photosynthetic pigments, they used carbon dioxide, water, and solar energy to produce carbohydrates for their growth, replication, and diversification and released oxygen as a by-product. Thus by using different approaches to harness solar energy, plant evolution resulted in the dominance and diversity of plant forms and contributed to the development of an oxygenated atmosphere. Plant forms evolved from unicellular forms that flourished in an externally turbulent environment that brought them into contact with energy and mineral resources into multicellular plant forms that could control the physical turbulence initially in the oceans, and later on land. Multicellular plants were able to organize themselves so as to contain the turbulence internally in terms of water and nutrient movements between their roots, trunk, and leaves, and this allowed multicellular plants to colonize and flourish on land. Plants perform similar functions, and hence do not show considerable diversity compared with animals; however, they possess considerable plasticity in life form in that no two plants of the same species show identical rooting and branching structures. The composition of autotrophic microbes and plants (that is, synthesizers of organic matter) in any ecosystem determines the architecture of that ecosystem.

Animal life forms evolved subsequently, taking advantage of and depending on the prevailing autotrophs. Different approaches to the partitioning of energy from organic matter ingested by animals, that is, differential energy assimilation for basal metabolism, movement, storage as fat, investment in few or many offspring, excretion, predation, and parasitism, permits the diversification of animal species. Animal species thus evolved over time from sedentary to mobile; from those without skeletons to those with an external skeleton (such as insects) and later an internal skeleton (for instance, vertebrates); from those adapted for an aquatic life to those adapted for a terrestrial, air breathing life; from those unable to regulate their body temperature (poikilothermic) to those that could do so (homoiothermic); and from those that produced thousands or millions of tiny offspring so that a few could survive to those that produced a few large young with a greater certainty of survival. This evolutionary trend was made possible by the centralization of the nervous system and the formation and evolution of the brain.

The link between a plant or a microbial species and an animal species constitutes an elementary food (or trophic) chain, one that exhibits complementarity of function and co-evolution between two different trophic levels. The success, that is, the survival, and regeneration of species in a food chain are determined by their efficient adaptation to specific functions and places or niches in an ecosystem in terms of their energy, nutrient, and habitat use, their accumulation of genetic or behavioral information over time, and their dynamics between trophic levels. Each species plays its own "game" with nature within each ecosystem boundary in developing a unique energy-partitioning strategy, that is, high metabolism, throughput, predation or parasitism, storage, growth, or reproduction. Some, such as hummingbirds and cheetahs, have a high maintenance strategy. Others, like weeds, herrings, and locusts, have a high reproductive strategy whereby they produce a large quantity of offspring with little investment in each, so that only a few will survive. Still others like palm and some rainforest trees, elephants, and whales have a high growth strategy, whereby they invest in large size and a few large offspring so as to ensure that most will survive. Dominant species have been those that are better able to store and use energy and/or information.

Human evolution has occurred relatively recently; however, rapid population growth and industrialization and high patterns of consumption, especially in the last 300 years, threaten the Earth's life-support systems and the sustainability of the biosphere as we know it. While in nature all populations, communities, and ecosystems function suboptimally because of resource scarcity and the need for reserves for unexpected events, the human species has tended to deviate from this pattern. In doing so, while human use and perturbation of habitats favors some species, others are threatened with extinction, in turn threatening the functioning of ecological processes on which human life depends. Thus humanity must move toward more sustainable paths of development, adapting its socioeconomic needs to the physical realities of the biosphere. Sustainable development is a dynamic balance between economic, ecological, and sociological imperatives and benefits over time, so that future generations will have the same potential and opportunities for human livelihood and development as current generations. Figure 3.1 illustrates the interaction necessary between economic, ecological, and social factors to attain sustainable development.

Figure 3.1.   *Interplay of Economic, Ecological, and Sociological Factors for Attaining Sustainable Development*

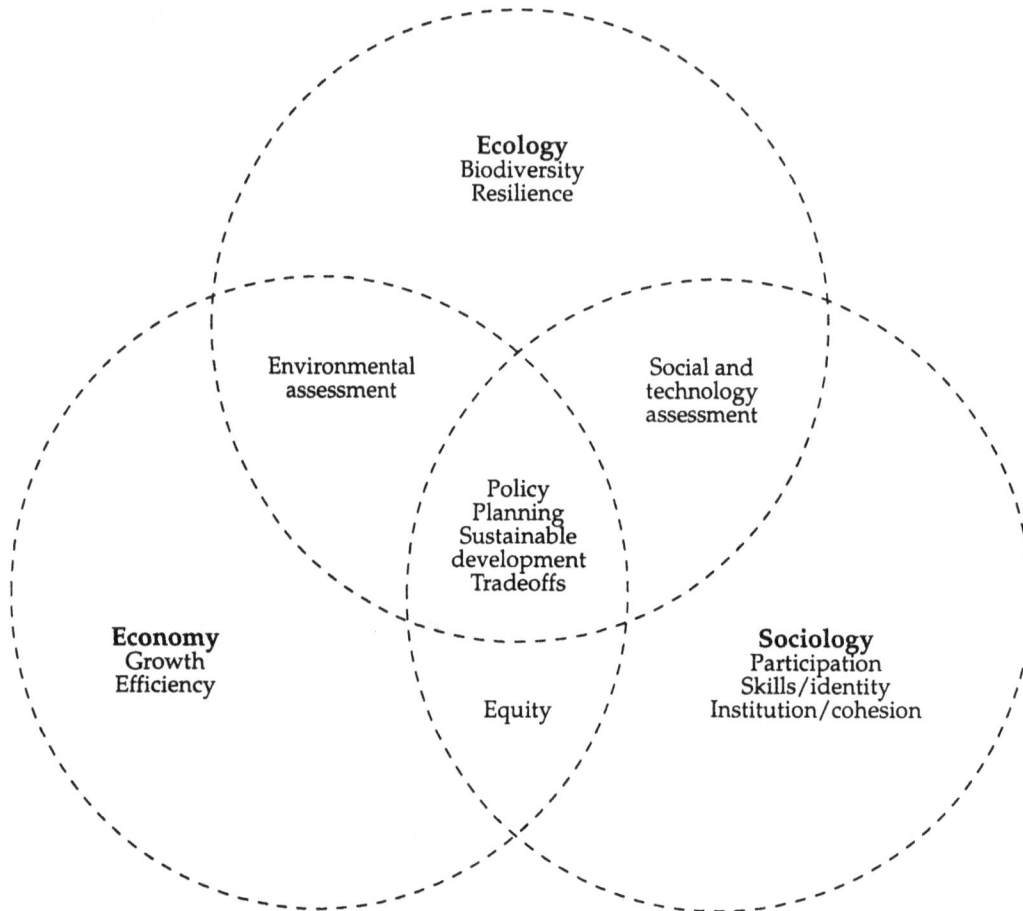

Source: Authors.

Ecological Processes Are Self-Organizing, and Energy Flow Leads to Complex Ecosystems

The structure and function of all ecosystems, whether natural or manmade, is determined by the following five principal resources or factors:

- Energy (or money)
- Materials
- Space
- Time
- Information (or knowledge).

Solar or external energy flows through two pathways in ecosystems. In the producer pathway, primary producers, that is, plants, fix energy from the sun and convert it to biomass. By eating plant biomass, plant eating organisms, such as grazing insects, fish, birds, and mammals, pass the energy to a higher trophic level, and, finally the energy passes through carnivorous insects, fish, amphibians, reptiles, birds, and mammals. In the decomposer pathway, with the help of thermal energy, dead organisms and nutrients contribute to a sequence that involves the breakdown of dead organic matter into smaller parts by insects and animals that specialize in eating dead organic matter (detritus). This is followed by a sequence of anaerobic breakdown involving fungi, bacteria, and microorganisms.

Several points that have direct consequences for environmental sustainability emerge from the energy flow in ecosystems and the resulting ecosystem structure. The first is that in mature ecosystems 50 percent of the energy flows through the grazing (producer) pathway, while the remainder flows through the detritus (decomposer) pathway. Conversely, in immature or simplified ecosystems, as in agro-ecosystems, as much as 70 percent of the energy may flow through the grazing pathway, thereby reducing the system's capacity to handle organic decomposition. In such systems, the soil microorganic life is not viable enough to provide an optimal decomposition process. This is a key factor for nutrient access by crops, and is a critical issue that modern agricultural systems need to address.

The second point is the inefficiency in energy conversion at each trophic level. Energy conversion is inefficient at each transformation when one organism is being eaten by another from a higher trophic level. The conversion efficiency at each stage is about 10 percent, being slightly higher among carnivores compared with herbivores and omnivores. This inefficiency implies that a food chain has at the most three or four links, rarely five, and the population of species at the lower trophic levels has to be larger than that at the higher levels. As a consequence of inefficient conversion between tropic levels, materials that are not easily metabolized, such as heavy metals and chlorinated hydrocarbons, accumulate in the food chain (a process known as bioaccumulation), which affects predator populations in particular.

Trophic links are only one way in which groups of species with common food needs are organized. Species are also associated by habitat requirements, strata (for instance, terrestrial or arboreal), patch mosaic (mosaic of different kinds of patches of grassland, tree stands, and so on), reproductive requirements, migratory or nonmigratory habits, alternation of generations (or a sexual generation alternating with an asexual generation), symbiosis, and proto-cooperation (or elementary cooperation). Mature ecosystems are characterized by highly complex interactions in which no single species is totally dependent on another, except for special forms of symbiosis and parasitism. Each species functions suboptimally. Perturbations and the elimination of predators and parasites result in simplified relationships. When a few species become absolutely dependent on one another in a simplified ecosystem, their relationships are potentially unstable in the face of external shocks, as in monocultures.

Ecological Processes Unfold in Systems Within Systems

The complexity and heterogeneity of ecosystems and the richness of biological diversity are overwhelming. Natural ecosystems comprise mosaics of heterogeneity created by physical (for instance, fire, storm) and biotic (for example, pest infestation, disease, treefall) events. These events influence the organizational building blocks of ecosystems. The following four ecological functions facilitate a process called succession, which is responsible for the changes in the structure of a particular part of an ecosystem over time and space:

- Exploitation by pioneer, opportunist species (r-species)
- Conservation and consolidation by climax species (k-species)
- Release of energy and nutrients
- Reorganization of nutrients and energy and accessible carbon.

Figure 3.2 illustrates the process of succession and the ecological functions involved. For example, consider what happens when an open area becomes available in a forest. The area is exploited first by pioneer species (r-species). These species have an opportunistic survival strategy of producing large numbers of young (r-strategy) and dispersing their seeds widely, and they can endure the heat of the sun. The outcome can be considered as an immature ecosystem. As the plants in the immature ecosystem grow, the amount of shade increases, and other plant species that are more sensitive to sunlight will start to grow. Over time, more light-sensitive species will take over, outgrowing the initial sun-loving plants, creating more shade, and forming a mature ecosystem. This stage is dominated by the function of conservation. Most of the nutrient and biomass capital is locked up in the system's plants, which prevents its use by other competitive species. Species with a lower investment in dispersal and a higher investment in

Figure 3.2.   *Ecosystem Processes*

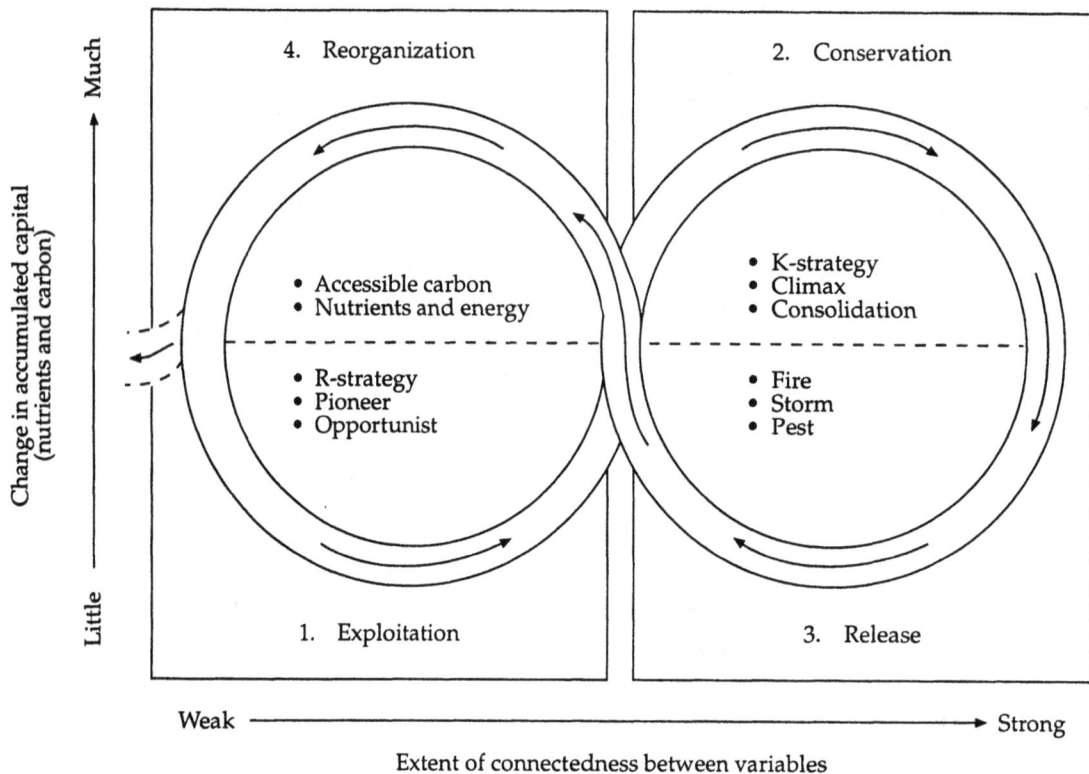

Source: Adapted from Holling and others (1995).

growth and consolidation (k-species) dominate this so-called climax ecosystem. At any time the climax system can face disturbance or destruction by biotic or abiotic sources, such as pest attack, a fire, or a storm. When this occurs, nutrients and carbon are released, thereby permitting reorganization in the system. After excessive release of nutrients and carbon, processes in the soil are responsible for the reorganization function, whereby nutrients can be mobilized and become available for exploitation, thereby closing the process of succession.

Where environments are fairly stable, such as at the equator and deep in the ocean, ecosystems tend to have a rich diversity, and where environments fluctuate, as in temperate zones, ecosystems have low diversity. However, temperate ecosystems tend to be more resilient than wet tropical ones because of the natural climatic fluxes they experience.

Another aspect of the hierarchical structure of ecosystems is the food web. Mature ecosystems have complex food webs and considerable elasticity for persisting during adverse conditions, while immature ecosystems have simple food chains and have less elasticity to persist under adverse conditions. The relationships between species in a food web involve competition between species at a higher trophic level (predators, parasites) for species at a lower level (prey, hosts). These relationships help maintain ecological checks and balances.

Ecosystems Vary in Their Absorption and Regeneration Capacity Relative to Human Disturbance

Every species and ecosystem has its unique features, and each exhibits a particular response to stress from external factors, such as human-induced disturbance. Most species and ecosystems have tolerance levels at which they can survive stress, such as contamination by heavy metals or large harvest levels, but they all have a point at which they pass the tolerance threshold and degenerative processes start. These threshold levels, or optimum levels of tolerance or production, are referred to as the maximum sustainable yield.

The maximum sustainable yield of a single-species resource, for instance, fish or timber, is defined as that yield that can be sustained with a given or increasing harvesting effort over time (figure 3.3). If more of a resource such as fish is harvested than the maximum sustainable yield, populations will decline over time, because their regenerative capacity will have been exceeded. Given the unique characteristics of every species and ecosystem, a number of factors determine the maximum sustainable yield. This implies that making generalizations about the responses of different ecosystems is difficult, and each case must be studied in its local context. All species, habitats, communities, and ecosystems exhibit an inverted U-shaped relationship between their productivity and the intensity of harvesting or waste discharge in the environment, whether measured in terms of biomass yield or waste assimilation capacity. That is, species, habitats, ecosystems, and environmental media usually function suboptimally. They increase their metabolism with usage or inputs up to an ecological optimum, beyond which they regress, and during this process they simplify the structure and dynamics of the system concerned. The relationship between productivity and the intensity of use is unique to renewable biological resources and environmental media. In contrast, the productivity of pervasive universal resources, for instance, electromagnetism, gravity, and radiation, remains constant with use; that of nonrenewable resources, such as minerals and fossil materials, decreases with use; and the productivity of information and knowledge increases with use.

The maximum sustainable yield was the origin of the sustainability concept. Initially it was used for the harvesting of a single-species resource, but was later expanded to tropical forestry systems, agro-

Figure 3.3. *Productivity Capacity of Different Types of Resources*

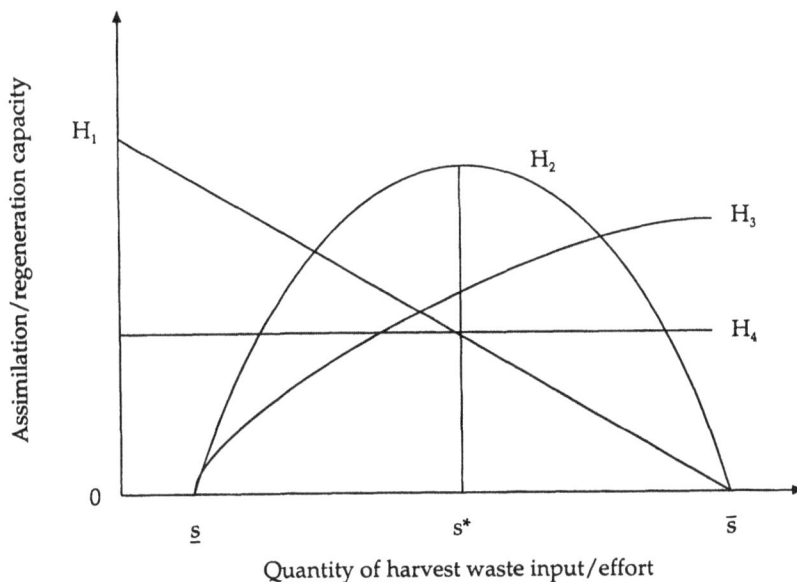

H_1 Nonrenewable resources.
H_2 Renewable resources and environmental media.
H_3 Information and knowledge.
H_4 Pervasive universal resources.
$\underline{s}$ Minimum viable stock.
$\bar{s}$ Natural equilibrium stock.
s^* Maximum sustainable yield.
Source: Authors.

ecosystems, and ecosystems, and eventually to the combination of biophysical and socioeconomic systems. In this sense, sustainability advocates that humanity should strive to coexist with nature.

Ecosystems Comprise the Sum of Ecological Processes, Which Exceeds the Sum of Objects or Species

Natural ecosystems perform four types of functions as follows:

- Regulatory functions essential for ecological processes and life-support systems, such as clean air, water, and soil
- Carrier functions that provide space and substrate for human livelihoods, for example, habitation, cultivation, and recreation
- Production functions that provide resources for human needs, such as food, raw materials, energy, and genetic materials
- Information functions that provide opportunities for human reflection, spiritual enrichment, cognitive development, and aesthetic experience, including the maintenance of human health.

All these functions are the result of the sum of a range of ecological processes that encompass the physical and biological elements of ecosystems. The resulting services provided add up to much more than the sum of individual objects or species. It is the interrelationships and the physical environment that constitute ecosystems.

All Ecological Processes Are Interrelated

The first four axioms of ecosystems outlined earlier all imply and lead up to the overarching axiom of ecology: all ecological processes are interrelated, and thus every part of the system is interdependent upon other parts, whether directly or indirectly. On a large scale, no air breathing organisms, such as humans, could exist without the plants that produce oxygen through photosynthesis. On a small scale, species interact and depend on other species. Dependence can be direct and strong, as in the case of symbiotic relationships among lichens or in coral reefs, or the interaction can be more indirect, like when one species constitutes one of many possible food sources for another species.

Policy Implications of the Axioms

To achieve environmental sustainability, development policies and technologies need to pay special attention to the following:

- Integrating the valuation of natural resources in planning. Scientists have identified 52 ecological processes that ecosystems provide, 37 of which they have classified in accordance with the four major types of functions outlined earlier and valued using economic approaches. These valuations are a vital step in facilitating the mainstreaming of environmental aspects into policy decisions.
- Maintaining continuous awareness that ecosystems and the biodiversity supporting them have not been valued holistically. The added value of the diverse parts of ecosystems may continue to evade economic valuation and must therefore be considered in their own right.
- Retaining the structure of natural ecosystems so that they may retain genetic information, which is important for biodiversity conservation and protected area systems, and can grow and adapt to changing external conditions.
- Focusing on the trophic dynamics and connectivity within ecosystems so that they are not simplified to the point that they lack interspecific competition at any level, or that one species is completely dependent on only one other, thereby making the system unstable, for example, vulnerable to disease, such as in intensive monoculture of shrimp, poultry, or crops.
- Taking into consideration the ease with which less resilient ecosystems are affected by perturbations, such as eutrophication (nutrient enrichment), overfishing, and overexploitation.

- Being aware of the considerable uncertainty about the effects of large-scale environmental changes, such as the fragmentation of landscapes by agriculture and urbanization. The remaining habitats for different organisms may be too small to support viable populations.
- Minimizing waste, recycling, and never exceeding the assimilative capacity of ecosystems.
- Avoiding substances that organisms find difficult or impossible to break down (metabolize) and that can therefore accumulate in species and persist in the environment for long periods. To devise the right policies, monitoring contamination by such chemicals is essential. This can be done by using top predators or especially sensitive species as indicators of ecological health and measuring the concentration of persistent substances in their bodies, as well as the negative effects they have on their health and survival.
- Preventing unexpected consequences because of events in one part of the ecosystem, such as global warming or acid precipitation.
- Realizing that ecosystems will continue evolving with or without *Homo sapiens*.

A basic knowledge of the character of ecological, environment, and social relationships can help policymakers understand the limitations of ecosystems to absorb the consequences of economic activities.

Conclusion

Ecological processes follow certain axioms that set the rules for how ecosystems function and how they respond to stress, such as disturbances caused by economic activities. Ecosystems can tolerate stress to varying degrees. In their natural state they are usually not functioning at their optimum level of either production or assimilation capacity, but all have a point beyond which degenerative processes start. When degeneration proceeds this far, the level of energy and capital inputs needed to rehabilitate the system will increase.

Thus the most cost-effective approach is to make every effort not to go beyond the optimum tolerance level, which implies trying to prevent environmental problems rather than trying to correct them after they have occurred. Such efforts will call for a profound understanding of the fundamental ecological axioms, combined with thorough knowledge of the local resource and ecosystem in question. However, in the final policy analysis, there may not be enough detailed knowledge to foresee all possible consequences of a policy, project, or program accurately. Policymakers need to acknowledge the level of uncertainty that remains and deal with it to their best ability. In such situations of uncertainty, some guiding principles for political decisions are valuable (see chapter 2 in this volume). Among these is the precautionary principle that warrants extreme care and mitigation efforts if the potential effects of a policy are far-reaching and irreversible.

References

Holling, C. S., D. W. Schindler, B. H. Walker, and J. Roughgarden. 1995. "Biodiversity in the Functioning of Ecosystems: An Ecological Synthesis." In C. Folke, C. S. Holling, B. O. Jansson, and K. G. Maler, eds., *Bilogical Diversity: Economic and Social Issues*. Cambridge, U.K.: Cambridge University Press.

Other Recommended Readings

Dasgupta, P., C. Folke, and Karl-Goran Maler. 1994. "The Environmental Resource Base and Human Welfare." In Kerstin Lindahl-Kiessling and Hans Landberg, eds., *Population, Economic Development, and the Environment*. Oxford, U.K.: Oxford University Press.

Folke, C., and T. Kaberer, eds. 1991. *Linking the Natural Environment and the Economy*. Dordrecht, Netherlands: Kluwer Academic.

4

The Dynamics of Creating and Maintaining Wealth

While the Brundtland Commission defined sustainable development in terms of meeting the needs of future generations, recognition that these needs may not be comparable across countries and across time is growing. An emerging and powerful interpretation of sustainable development concentrates on preserving and enhancing the opportunities open to people in countries worldwide (Serageldin 1994). From this viewpoint, shifting attention from flow measures of economic activity, such as gross national product (GNP), to stocks of environmental resources, produced assets, and human resources, is crucial. Stocks of wealth underpin the opportunities available to people, and the process of sustaining development is fundamentally the process of creating, maintaining, and managing wealth.

One particular component of the wealth of nations—social capital—is both important and difficult to value. Social capital may be roughly conceived of as the set of norms, networks, and organizations through which people gain access to power and resources and through which decisionmaking and policy formulation occur. While this chapter does not present empirical estimates of social capital, it does explore many of the conceptual issues and implications for development policy.

Armed with better measures of wealth, refining our measures of income and savings to guide the actions of decisionmakers whose objective is to achieve sustainable development is then possible. Income adjusted for depletion and degradation of the environment is sometimes referred to as the eco-domestic product (or green gross domestic product), while the corresponding savings measure is termed genuine savings (World Bank 1997).

Expanded Wealth Accounts

The analysis of sustainable development requires a suitably expansive definition of wealth. At a minimum, wealth should include produced assets, human capital, natural resources, and liabilities in the form of stocks of pollution. This goes far beyond the usual confines of national accounting and introduces new challenges in both theory and measurement. While expanded wealth accounts should include the value of social capital, arriving at empirical estimates of the economic returns to social capital is extremely difficult in practice. We therefore combine social capital with human capital in a composite human resources category.

The World Bank (1997) presents wealth estimates for nearly 100 countries, broken down as follows:

- *Natural capital* is estimated as the sum of the stock value of the following renewable and nonrenewable resources: agricultural land, pasture land, timber, nontimber forest benefits, protected areas, oil, coal, natural gas, metals, and minerals.
- *Produced assets* are the sum of the value of a country's stock of machinery and equipment, buildings, and infrastructure.
- *Human resources* represent the stock value of all economic returns that cannot be attributed to either human or produced assets. This therefore implicitly values the wealth inherent in raw labor, human capital, and social capital together.

Based on presentations by John Dixon, Kirk Hamilton, and Vinod Thomas.

Not surprisingly, empirical estimates of wealth indicate that the human resource component is the most important constituent. As table 4.1 shows, human resources account for the main share of wealth, from 40 to 80 percent, in all regions of the world.

The measurement of the wealth of nations in total and its components is largely motivated by concerns about sustainable development. While this is important in itself, given the commitments that the World Bank and its client countries have made to achieve environmentally sustainable development, it also suggests a new model for economic development: development as portfolio management, that is, the process of transforming an endowment of assets so as to achieve development objectives. This contrasts with the traditional approach to development, which emphasizes the building of infrastructure.

Eco-Domestic Product

After World War II, the main objective for countries around the globe was to rebuild their shattered economies. The system of national accounts was developed around that time, and not surprisingly, it focused only on measuring economic growth, in particular, production in markets. At that time, resources were seen as abundant, and the environment as an inexhaustible sink. This perception no longer holds, and countries increasingly seek to take the degradation of the environment into account. In response to this growing concern, the United Nations (1993) published its handbook on a *System of integrated Environmental and Economic Accounts*. The measure of income that is defined in the handbook is the eco-domestic product, which contrasts with gross domestic product, the traditional national accounting aggregate. The eco-domestic product is defined as follows:

eco-domestic product = gross domestic product – depreciation of produced assets
– depletion of natural resources – degradation and pollution damage

If policymakers are to have a true picture of the rate of economic progress, they must have better and more encompassing measures of national income. Viewed in this light, the eco-domestic product is intrinsically important. From the viewpoint of sustainability, however, the eco-domestic product is only one step in the right direction: while it provides a truer measure of income, it does not directly measure whether this income can be sustained. This is the motivation for defining genuine savings.

Table 4.1.   *Wealth by Geographic Region, 1994*

Region	US$ per capita				Percentage of total wealth		
	Total wealth	Human resources	Produced assets	Natural capital	Human resources	Produced assets	Natural capital
North America	326,000	249,000	62,000	16,000	76	19	5
Pacific OECD	302,000	205,000	90,000	8,000	68	30	2
Western Europe	237,000	177,000	55,000	6,000	74	24	2
Middle East	150,000	65,000	27,000	58,000	43	18	39
South America	95,000	70,000	16,000	9,000	74	17	9
North Africa	55,000	38,000	14,000	3,000	69	26	5
Central America	52,000	41,000	8,000	3,000	79	15	6
Caribbean	48,000	33,000	10,000	5,000	69	20	11
East Asia	47,000	36,000	7,000	4,000	77	15	8
East and Southern Africa	30,000	20,000	7,000	3,000	66	25	10
West Africa	22,000	13,000	4,000	5,000	60	18	21
South Asia	22,000	14,000	4,000	4,000	65	19	16

OECD Organisation for Economic Co-operation and Development.
Source: World Bank (1997).

Genuine Savings

The traditional measure of a nation's rate of accumulation of wealth is gross saving, calculated as GNP minus public and private consumption. Gross saving represents the total amount of produced output that is set aside for the future in the form either of foreign lending or of investments in productive assets. However, gross savings rates say little about the sustainability of development, both because of the normal depreciation of produced assets, and because of the depletion and degradation of the environment that are a byproduct of economic activity.

Wealth represents the potential to generate income or, more broadly, to generate welfare. Changes in wealth are therefore intimately linked to the question of sustainability, and the notion of genuine savings can most simply be conceived of as the net change in wealth over an accounting period as new assets are invested, old assets depreciate, and natural resources are augmented or depleted. As both theory and common sense dictate, negative rates of genuine savings imply that a country is not on a sustainable path.

The accounting relationships for genuine savings can be seen in figure 4.1, which shows the components of genuine savings as shares of GNP for Tunisia. The calculation begins with standard national accounting. The top curve in figure 4.1 is gross domestic investment, that is, total investment in structures, equipment, and inventory accumulation. Gross saving is obtained by subtracting net foreign borrowing (including net official transfers) from gross domestic investment. Next, the depreciation of produced assets is deducted, yielding the curve for net saving. Finally, the bottom line is genuine savings, which is obtained by subtracting the value of resource depletion and pollution damages from net savings.

Resource depletion is measured as the total rents on resource extraction and harvesting. For each natural resource, rents are estimated as the difference between the value of production at world prices

Figure 4.1.   Genuine Savings for Tunisia, 1970–94

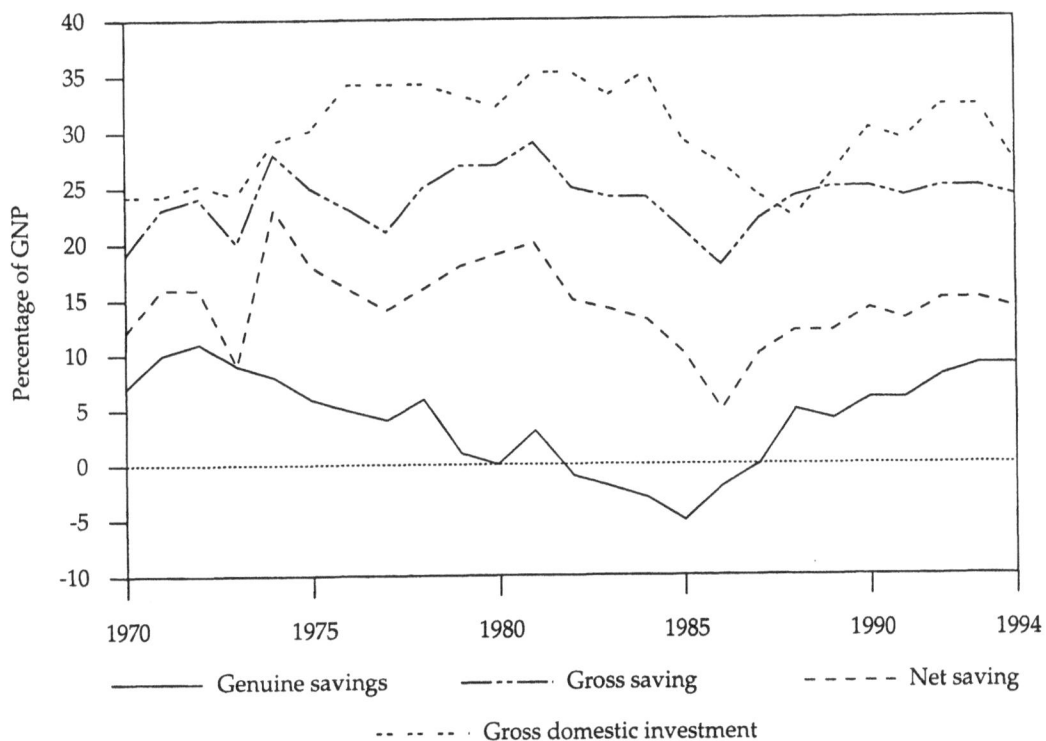

Source: World Bank (1997, p. 31).

and the total costs of production, including depreciation of fixed assets and return on capital. Strictly speaking, this measures economic profits on extraction rather than scarcity rents, and for technical reasons this gives an upward bias to the value of depletion (and a downward bias to genuine savings).

Forest resources enter the depletion calculation as the difference between the rental value of roundwood harvests and the corresponding value of natural growth, both in forests and in plantations. A depletion charge is entered for a country when the amount of wood harvested exceeds natural growth. Therefore, this valuation captures the commercial value of forests, but fails to capture the other services trees provide, the nontimber values.

Pollution damage enters green national accounts in several ways. Even though damage to produced assets (for instance, damage to buildings caused by acid rain) does appear in depreciation figures in theory, in practice, most of such damage is not picked up. Standard national accounts already reflect the effects of pollution on output (damage to crops, lost production due to morbidity), but not explicitly. The key pollution adjustment is therefore for welfare effects, and values the willingness to pay to avoid excess mortality and the pain and suffering caused by morbidity brought about by pollution.

Recent estimates of genuine savings at the World Bank have also included current expenditures on education as a type of investment in human capital. This involves reclassifying the current private and public expenditures on education as investment rather than consumption (the figures are reported in World Bank 1999).

A calculation of average genuine savings rates as a percentage of GNP for the various regions of the world during 1970–94 reveals striking differences. In many developing regions, decisive moments in economic performance are reflected in large movements in the genuine savings rate (figure 4.2). The

Figure 4.2. *Genuine Savings Rates by Region, 1970–94*

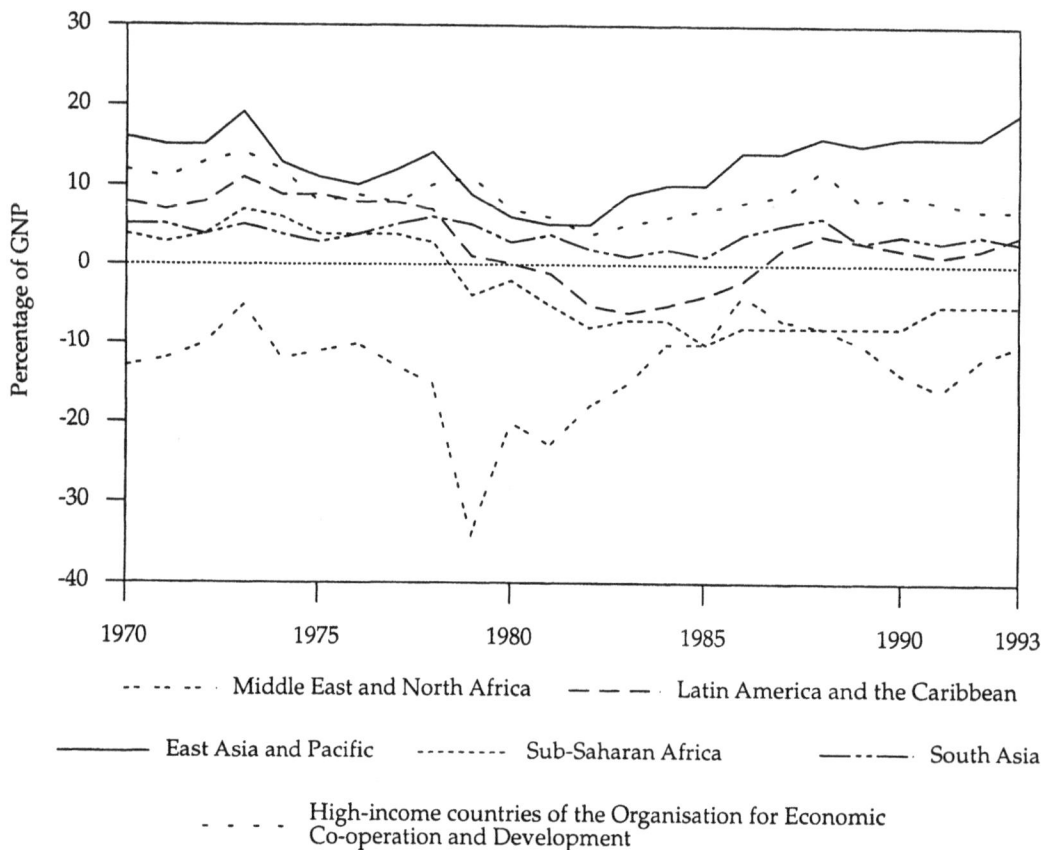

- -- -- -- Middle East and North Africa   — — — Latin America and the Caribbean

———— East Asia and Pacific   - - - - - - - - Sub-Saharan Africa   —--— South Asia

- - - -   High-income countries of the Organisation for Economic
          Co-operation and Development

Source: World Bank (1997, pp. 31, 33).

figure also reveals a disappointing trend for the countries of Sub-Saharan Africa, where average genuine savings rates exceeded 5 percent of GNP around the mid-1970s, fell sharply at the end of the 1970s, and have never recovered. Despite a slight recovery in the early 1990s, regional genuine dissaving has recently been near 7 percent. Equally important, negative genuine savings rates have been accompanied by persistently low regional indicators of human welfare, including education, nutrition, and medical care (World Bank 1996a).

The oil crisis coincided with a period of decline in genuine savings throughout Latin America and the Caribbean, where figures had previously stood at some 8 to 9 percent of GNP. In 1982, the year of Mexico's debt crisis, regional genuine savings dropped to negative 5 percent. As the area has emerged from debt crisis, returned to democratic rule, and spurred the vigorous growth of the "jaguars," genuine savings rates have shown a consistently positive trend, but remain, well below 5 percent of GNP.

In contrast, until 1994 the East Asia and Pacific region had exhibited genuine savings rates topping 15 percent of GNP. Although these countries also suffered at the time of the oil crisis, high genuine savings rates since that time have mirrored the outstanding economic performance of these countries. The recent financial crisis in this region underscores an important point, however; namely, while genuine savings can indicate the true saving effort in a country or region, it is only one indicator among the many that are required to assess whether the country is vulnerable to economic shocks.

The Middle East and North Africa region stands out because of its consistently negative genuine savings. Total consumption as a share of GNP rose from around 50 percent in the 1970s to more than 70 percent by the end of the 1980s, and imports of food and manufactured goods flowed into the region as many current account surpluses of the 1970s turned into deficits in the 1980s (World Bank 1996b). However, the foregoing caveats about upward biases in depletion estimates need to be taken into account when examining the figures, because as the most resource-dependent economies, these countries will exhibit the highest downward bias as a share of GNP in estimated genuine savings rates.

South Asia exhibited moderately positive rates of genuine savings during the period. This is consistent with the moderate rates of economic growth that have characterized the countries of the region.

Finally, rates of genuine savings in the high-income countries of the Organisation for Economic Cooperation and Development, pushed upward by high investment, relatively less dependence on natural resources, and strong exports of high value added goods and services, were near 10 percent for much of the period under review. The 1982/83 and 1990 recessions coincided with downward turns in genuine savings rates, but the figures consistently exhibit an absence of volatility and large rates of genuine dissaving seen in other regions.

Social Capital

When dealing with sustainable development issues, the three traditional types of capital (natural, physical, and human) can only partially explain the process of economic growth. Another important aspect of economic growth is the way in which economic actors interact and organize themselves to generate growth and development. The missing link is social capital. Because of the difficulties inherent in identifying and valuing social capital, it has been neglected not only in national accounts, but also in policy discussions. Nevertheless, it plays a critical role in the accumulation of wealth.

Social capital concerns the informal and formal institutions that govern the actions of individuals within a society. Debate about precisely what elements should be included in social capital is ongoing. Some say that social capital only includes social networks, that is, horizontal associations among people, while others claim that it encompasses the social structure at large and the norms and values that govern human interaction. The broadest definition of social capital integrates the social and political environments that facilitate development. According to this definition, social capital includes formal structures and institutions, governments, political regimes, judiciary systems, and political and civil liberties. These definitions should be seen as complementary, because the evidence increasingly shows that all these items influence economic growth, equity, and poverty alleviation. (For discussions of various definitions of social capital see, for example, Putnam 1993; World Bank 1997.)

Benefits and Costs of Social Capital

The costs involved in building social capital are largely unknown for the reasons mentioned previously. Current work strives to operationalize the definition of social capital and to calculate possible costs. Table 4.2 shows some of the indicators of social capital that have been used. Cross-country comparisons of these indicators have revealed the role of social capital. For example, higher levels of trust and civil associations were conducive to growth, especially in the poorest countries; World Bank-financed projects in countries where civic liberties were high have shown much higher economic returns; and other elements of social capital demonstrated to be highly correlated with growth are contract enforcement, risk of expropriation, corruption, and quality of government bureaucracy.

In addition to contributing to economic growth, social capital also improves the quality of life. Strong social networks create a sense of unity and a stable and functioning government provides an element of security to a society. However, social relationships can be used for beneficial or detrimental outcomes, for instance, either for improving cooperation and equity in development or for improving the efficiency of criminal networks (World Bank 1997). Social capital is a valuable asset, but like all kinds of capital it can be misused.

Functions of Social Capital

One way in which social capital contributes to creating wealth is by increasing the amount of information and knowledge available for decisionmaking. When making decisions, actors try to take into account both the immediate and the future consequences of those decisions. They are much better off the more they know about how different characteristics of their society will influence those consequences. For instance, if people want to buy a piece of property, they will try to find out as much as possible about the legal status of that property. If they buy it now, can they be sure that future governments will perceive the contract as valid? Can they depend on a fair bidding process for the property that gives them an equal opportunity to that of others to buy it? The existence of social capital in the form of a stable legal system with secure property rights and validity of contracts increases the level of information about the future and helps in economic decisionmaking. That is, when they can trust the institutional system, people will know that when they buy a property they will be able to retain it for the foreseeable future and be sure that pertinent contracts are binding.

The ways in which social capital affects economic growth in broader terms can be summarized as the building of trust in institutions (formal and informal) and in people, which facilitates cooperative

Table 4.2. Some Indicators of Social Capital

Horizontal associations and cooperation	Social cohesion	Governance and political and civil society
Number and type of associations/ local institutions	Indicator of social mobility	Independence of court system
Extent of membership	Measure of strength of "social tensions"	Expropriation/nationalization risk
Extent of participatory decisionmaking	Ethnolinguistic fragmentation	Contract enforceability
Extent of income/occupational diversity	Homicide rate	Index of civil liberties
Homogeneity within association	Suicide rate	Index of intensity of political or economic discrimination
	Other crime rates	
Extent of trust in village	Youth unemployment rate	Strength of democratic institutions
Members/government		Degree of decentralization of government

Source: Adapted from World Bank (1997, p. 85).

decisionmaking and action. For example, trusting formal institutions can entail trusting in the validity of contracts, of formal and informal agreements, of the legal system, and of basic property laws; and trusting informal institutions can entail trusting in a common value system, in social codes of action, in nongovernmental decisionmaking, and in enforcement systems (self-regulation). Trust becomes easier to develop if institutions provide individuals with incentives to follow a system's rules and regulations. Thus institutions have to incorporate enforcement mechanisms that give people incentives to conform to expected behavior and not misuse the system, because those who break contracts face sanctions.

Informal Institutions and Collective Actions

In situations where coordinated action outside the formal government is beneficial or necessary, informal institutions can both facilitate the switch from independent to collective decisionmaking and help ensure that most actors will conform to agreed decisions. An example of such a situation is when people must manage a local resource as common property. A common property resource is a resource that is owned neither privately nor by the state. This type of property rights regime implies that resource ownership and management is in the hands of an identifiable group of individuals who can exclude others and regulate use of the resource. In cases where such resources are locally confined, such as rangeland, a fishing bay, or a forest, local communities have often managed them well. Much research has been carried out to identify the factors that determine successful common property resource management. One such factor is that actors need to switch from independent to coordinated action, which they can do within a local organization created specifically to manage the resource in question. Studies have shown that to achieve success, members of such an organization must have (Ostrom 1992)

- Common understanding of the problem
- Common understanding of alternatives for coordination
- Common perceptions that decisionmaking costs do not exceed benefits
- Common perceptions of mutual trust and reciprocity.

These factors confirm the important role of social capital in a society that is faced with complex management issues that necessitate collective action.

Role of Values

Social norms of acceptable behavior are often based on some common value held in a society. Naturally, the kinds of values that dominate determine whether they are likely to contribute to the development of national wealth or not. Adherence to values that uphold the principles of equality, consideration for others, trustworthiness, service, compassion, and justice undoubtedly have a direct positive influence on wealth creation and a negative influence on the level of corruption, crime, and other factors that would hinder the building of sustainable national wealth.

If most people in a society adhere to some of these fundamental values, the economic gains could be substantial, because they would depend less on costly formal institutions. The stronger the trust that exists in informal institutions, the less costly will decisionmaking, monitoring, and enforcement processes be. Monitoring and enforcement mechanisms can either work through formal institutions, with legal or monetary sanctions for breaking the rules, or through informal systems, where pressure from the social network or an individual's conscience deters people from breaking the rules.

Development of Trust

Thus, as previously discussed, the productivity of social capital increases by increasing the level of trust among actors and toward institutions. Building social capital is similar to other activities where positive externalities exist, and governments definitely have a role to play in the building of such capital. Therefore, an important issue is what aspects of a society contribute to the building of trust.

The building of trust in a society is more likely to occur if social networks are horizontal rather than vertical and are built on kinship ties. Building trust is easier in settings where decisionmaking tends to be collective. In addition, a higher degree of equity in economic terms among actors facilitates the building of trust. Another factor that facilitates the building of trust is social cohesion. In a situation of social cohesion emotional bonds of loyalty exist between members that increase their inclination to focus on the well-being of the whole group. When no cohesion exists, society falls apart, not only in economic terms, but in social and human terms as well. The existence of cohesion in a society depends significantly on the kinds of values that predominate, for example, values that encourage consideration for others facilitate the building of cohesion. Instead of seeking personal goals, individuals focus on the broader goals of the group. That is, group utility has, to some extent, replaced personal utility.

Thus policymakers need to discover ways to encourage the development of values that contribute to societal cohesion. One way is through education, which can emphasize the values of global awareness, equality, and service to the community

Integrating Genuine Savings, Human Capital, and Social Capital into Policy

An integrated approach to analyzing physical, natural, human, and social capital can significantly assist decisionmaking that involves tradeoffs between different sectors. Sustainable development does not mean investing in environmental conservation to the detriment of other economic activities. It means looking at the mix of capital in a country and trying to achieve the optimal use of the different components that form a nation's wealth.

If traditional national accounting figures are modified to reflect the values of a broader range of assets, the importance of natural and human capital immediately becomes evident, even with incomplete measures of wealth and genuine savings. These indicators can become a powerful tool to convince policymakers and society at large of the need for sound natural and human resource development policies. If negative trends in genuine savings prevail, this should signal policymakers that national assets are being consumed and that policy reforms are required.

The development of human capital is critical for economic growth, poverty reduction, and sustained competitiveness in the export market. Thus a key question to address is how to invest in human capital. Evidence from East Asia suggests that policymakers should focus on providing high-quality primary and secondary education. Because education is also one of the factors that enable breaking the cycle of poverty, population growth, and environmental degradation (see chapter 6), governments should have strong incentives to invest heavily in education and capacity building to strengthen human capital (Thomas and Wang 1998).

The policy implications of social capital can affect such fundamental aspects of a society's structure as its legal system, its level of decentralization, and its extent of poverty and equity. Thus policy discussions need to encompass overarching approaches to governance systems. Apart from what the government can do in terms of designing formal institutions, it can play an important role in supporting informal institutions by, for example, lending authority and assistance to local nongovernmental associations and encouraging education systems to address values.

Conclusion

Fresh ways to view produced, natural, and human capital can assist in understanding the variety of factors that affect development. Quantitative work shows that while produced assets and natural resources are important, often the bulk of a nation's wealth rests in its human resources (the sum of human and social capital). From this expanded wealth measure we can derive more inclusive measures of income (eco-domestic product) and savings. Genuine savings, in turn, provides an indicator of sustainability.

In addition to the three major forms of capital that can be measured, another influential component of wealth is social capital. Social capital can significantly promote or hinder sustainable development activities, and its formation originates from both individuals in civil society and government institutions. It contributes to development by generating a certain level of trust in institutions and people that is needed for decisionmaking at all levels, and particularly for situations that call for coordinated action.

By themselves physical, natural, human, or social capital are not guarantees of economic development. It is the combination of all four types of capital and their efficient use that lays the foundation for sustained economic development.

References

Kunte, A., K. Hamilton, J. Dixon, and M. Clemens. 1998. *Estimating National Wealth: Methodology and Results.* Environmental Economics Series no.57. Washington D.C.: World Bank.

Ostrom, Elinor. 1992. " The Rudiments of a Theory of the Origins, Survival, and Performance of Common Property Institutions." In D. W. Bromley, ed., *Making the Commons Work: Theory, Practice, and Policy.* San Francisco: Institute for Contemporary Studies.

Putnam, Robert D. 1993. "The Prosperous Community: Social Capital and Public Life: The American Prospect." *Current* (356).

Seradeldin, Ismail. 1994. "Sustainability and the Wealth of Nations: First Steps in an Ongoing Journey." Paper distributed at the Third Annual International Conference on Environmentally Sustainable Development, World Bank, Washington, D.C.

Thomas, V., and Y. Wang. 1998. "Policy Links of East Asia: Openness, Education, and the Environment." Unpublished. World Bank, Washington D.C.

United Nations. 1993. *System of Integrated Environmental and Economic Accounts*World Bank. 1996a. *Economic and Social Database.* Washington, D.C.: International Economics Department.

_____. 1996b. *World Development Report 1996: From Plan to Market.* New York: Oxford University Press.

_____. 1997. *Expanding the Measure of Wealth: Indicators of Environmentally Sustainable Development.* Washington, D.C.

_____. 1999. *World Development Indicators 1999.* Washington, D.C.

Other Recommended Readings

Hamilton, K., and E. Lutz. 1996. *Green National Accounts: Policy Uses and Empirical Evidence.* Environmental Economic Series no. 039. Washington, D.C.: World Bank.

North, D. 1990. *Institutions, Institutional Change, and Economic Performance.* New York: Cambridge University Press.

Olson, M. 1982. *The Rise and Decline of Nations: Economic Growth, Stagflation, and Social Rigidities.* New Haven, Connecticut: Yale University Press

Ostrom, E. 1990. *Governing the Commons, the Evolution of Institutions for Collective Action.* New York: Cambridge University Press.

5

Institutions for Environmental Stewardship

Institutional factors and public participation are important for both the design and implementation of environmental policies. Without a well-functioning, formal system of institutions to support an environmental strategy, good designs will not be translated into reality. Similarly, without public input into policy design and implementation, policies intended to achieve a more equitable society are less likely to be developed. A substantial part of the implementation of sound environmental management practices depends critically on the public at the grassroots level and on active involvement by the public.

Conventionally, environmental management consists of priority setting, policymaking, coordination and implementation of policies, and monitoring and evaluation. The implementation of policy includes developing legislation, administrative structures, and an information base; creating regulatory and enforcement institutions; providing needed skills; ensuring adequate financial resources; and decentralizing some tasks to more effective local bodies.

Developing the Knowledge Base

Developing the knowledge base consists of two broad aspects: accumulation of knowledge and diffusion of knowledge. The public sector, both international and national, has a comparative advantage in accumulating knowledge. It can do this by allocating resources to research and scientific institutions and by promoting key partnerships with the private sector. To attain the broad goals of sustainable development, countries need experts from a variety of backgrounds because of the multidisciplinary aspects of the issues. Equally important, countries should have the human and financial capacities to assess the applicability of internationally generated knowledge to local ecological, socioeconomic, and cultural circumstances.

Knowledge dissemination is also a critical component of environmental management, as people need to understand environmental problems and some of the priority issues. Economists characterize many forms of environment and natural resources as free goods, and hence individuals can have direct impacts on the quality of these goods. Therefore, countries need to disseminate knowledge about the environment to a wide variety of stakeholders to promote sustainable resource management.

At the national level, policymakers must have open communication with the scientific community to ensure that research results with major policy implications are disseminated to policymakers and to the public at large. Government institutions are also well-served by keeping open channels for learning from local knowledge and from all stakeholder groups. The agriculture sector provides a clear example of how the knowledge of local smallholder farmers and their direct participation in both research and extension has greatly enhanced a sector's development.

With greater knowledge about the issues, policymakers will be better equipped to identify problems, discern available options, and assess their respective costs and benefits. Although striving toward more knowledge-based priority setting and action strategies does not free policymakers from the onus of making subjective choices, knowledge can make difficult, value-based decisions easier to arrive at.

Based on presentations by Tariq Banuri and Alfredo Sfeir-Younis.

Setting Priorities

Setting priorities among key environmental issues is important. Unfortunately, many governments have limited resources (financial, human, environmental capital, and so forth) available to them, and therefore need to establish priority areas for action. They should determine these areas based on the severity of a problem; the ability to resolve the problem, which depends on the level of technological and human capital available; the benefits associated with resolving the problem; and the costs of implementing the necessary measures.

Involving stakeholders, especially groups that are often marginalized such as women, the elderly, the poor, and the indigenous, in a consultative process to identify problems and set priorities will further widen policymakers perspectives about an issue and clarify conflicting priorities. Marginalized groups usually suffer the most from environmental threats, because they rely closely on natural resources and benefit the least from economic growth. An important aspect of the consultative process is that all participants should have a sense of shared interests, an acceptance of joint responsibility for the problem, and a willingness to contribute to its solution.

Subsequently, policymakers will have to reconcile local perceptions of problems with the data. For example, they need to know the number of people affected by a certain risk and the threat it poses to the environment. When this information is known, governments can prioritize among various environmental problems more easily than in the absence of such information. For example, in some cases, people may perceive problems to be more damaging to the environment than they actually are. Consider the case of litter. Many people believe that litter in the streets is a serious problem that requires immediate action; however, while unsightly, the health and environmental impacts of litter are limited compared with other urban problems, such as an insufficient supply of potable water, that have more serious implications for human health.

Building Consensus

Consensus building in setting priorities and making decisions is necessary at all levels—local, national, and international—and across levels. The diversity of views and priorities that exist within a society poses a substantial challenge to government institutions if the institutions are striving to arrive at publicly acceptable policies. Increased education to raise people's awareness of the issues is needed. This can be leveraged through the school system at the grassroots level and the media at the top levels of government, which is where financial resources are allocated. Access to relevant knowledge and priorities developed in a broad consultative process results in a higher probability that consensus will emerge around important policies.

Promoting Coordination

Environmental policy often cuts across ministerial and bureaucratic boundaries. For example, building a new dam would usually involve the ministries of agriculture, irrigation, natural resources, and energy. The first challenge is to achieve efficient coordination across ministries during the design phase. Attempting coordination at a later stage is likely to result in problems during implementation, because different agencies may already have developed their own policies, which might conflict with those of other agencies.

A failure on the part of government agencies to coordinate their activities is a common problem of projects and policies. One example is the city of São Paulo, Brazil. The metropolitan area has a planning agency, while state agencies are responsible for environmental protection, water, and sanitation. Responsibility is thus divided in a way whereby programs to control industrial pollution have not been integrated with investments in wastewater treatment. The state and metropolitan agencies have separate responsibilities that could be carried out more effectively if they took an integrated, cross-sectoral approach to policymaking.

Carrying out Implementation

Closing the gap between policymaking and implementation is essential. The World Bank's work in facilitating the development of national environmental action plans has shown that successful policy implementation has the following five main requirements (World Bank 1992):

- Clear legislative framework
- Appropriate administrative structure
- Technical skills
- Adequate financial resources
- Decentralized responsibility.

Legislative Framework

Laying the legal foundation for environmental management may mean reviewing existing laws, codifying new concepts, and drawing up detailed regulations. Straightforward legislation can clarify the rules of the game for the private sector by providing signals for operational strategies. If the rules are determined from the outset, this may give the private sector the necessary security to make investment decisions.

Administrative Structure

Institution building is a long-term process. It depends on local conditions and political factors and on the availability of human and financial capital. While each country's situation is unique, the test of a good administrative structure is its capacity to set priorities, coordinate actions, resolve conflicts, regulate activity, and enforce legislation. The following are some examples of such structures:

- Formal, high-level agencies that can provide advice on designing policy and monitoring implementation. Examples are the Brazil Environment Institute, the Federal Environment Protection Agency in Nigeria, and the State Environmental Protection Committee in China.
- Environmental units in the mainline ministries that can provide the central environmental unit with technical expertise and monitor those environmental policies that the ministries are responsible for implementing. For example, an environmental unit within the ministry of health may look after the public health aspect of environmental quality, whereas the management and conservation of natural resources may be spread among government units responsible for agriculture, forestry, fisheries, parks, and wildlife.

Technical Skills

Environmental management requires a mix of professional skills, such as natural or biological scientists, engineers, economists, and sociologists. However, the public sectors of many developing countries lack an adequate number of qualified staff at all levels. This is due to several reasons. First, salaries are low in the public sector. Second, hiring practices are biased toward technical skills as opposed to nontechnical specializations. Consequently, some countries finance foundations and institutes to fill the skills gap.

Financial Resources

Environmental agencies have not yet firmly established themselves in the competition for scarce government funds, while contributions from external donor agencies are frequently short term in nature. Some countries are making more money available for skilled technical staff, laboratories, and other monitoring devices as environmental management becomes accepted as an important objective. Long-term and reliable funding is necessary, especially for institution building and research.

Decentralization

Agencies, which are often short of human and financial capital, need to devise cost-effective ways to implement policy by means of decentralization. One alternative is for the government to delegate program implementation and/or monitoring to local communities or voluntary organizations. Japan has used this approach successfully, and many other countries are attempting to apply similar techniques. The private sector, nongovernmental organizations (NGOs), and community groups can also play a role in performing environmental assessments, collecting and analyzing data, undertaking monitoring and inspection, and providing specialized advice. For example, Mexico City is implementing air pollution control measures using private vehicle inspection stations, and is considering using private laboratories to analyze air and water samples.

Countries can achieve local involvement in environmental impact assessments by sharing information with local communities at early stages of project identification by discussing local concerns with affected communities, permitting public comments on background studies and draft environmental assessments, and including the results of hearings and comments in the final document.

Apart from voluntary organizations, the general public itself can be of valuable service to the government in implementing environmental policies. A good example is the Program for Pollution Control, Evaluation, and Rating (PROPER) in Indonesia, which uses an informational approach. The objective of this program is to reduce pollution by publicly disclosing pollution information. The government compiled information about 187 factories and then ranked the companies on their environmental stewardship. It gave heavily polluting firms six months to clean up. Failure to comply would have meant public disclosure of their pollution emissions. This has resulted in increased environmental awareness and clean up (Wheeler and Afsah 1996). Thus, sometimes simply obligating heavy polluters to publish information about their emissions can have a significant effect on their behavior. Educating the public about environmental concerns can also have a strong impact on pollution reduction, because public pressure can influence private businesses to use less-polluting techniques.

Examples are available from around the world where the public can contribute directly to afforestation, wildlife conservation, park management, improvements in sanitation systems and drainage, and flood control. Even though involving local people at the grassroots level is essential for implementing environmental policies, involving them in all stages of the policymaking process is equally critical.

Involving Local People

Involving the public in both the design and implementation stages of environmental management is critical for two major reasons. First, ethically and ideologically people should have the freedom to choose the direction of their own development and to influence the means by which they earn their livelihoods. Second, in recent decades development practitioners have come to realize that top-down development projects that clearly exclude stakeholders from the policymaking and implementation arena are detrimental to the success of these projects. World Bank evaluations of its own projects, as well as evaluations by the U.S. Agency for International Development of its projects, have repeatedly confirmed this (World Bank 1996). Figure 5.1 summarizes ways in which government institutions can promote participation, the effects participation has on development outcomes, and the political processes that represent a prerequisite for participation to take place.

Institutions Supporting Participation

If government institutions are to facilitate public and local participation by marginalized groups, the first requirement is the political will to bring about change. There must be a consensus to strive for decentralization in the different areas of environmental management and a genuine interest in involving all stakeholders.

Figure 5.1. Consensus Building in Environmental Management: The Role of the Public Sector and Civil Society

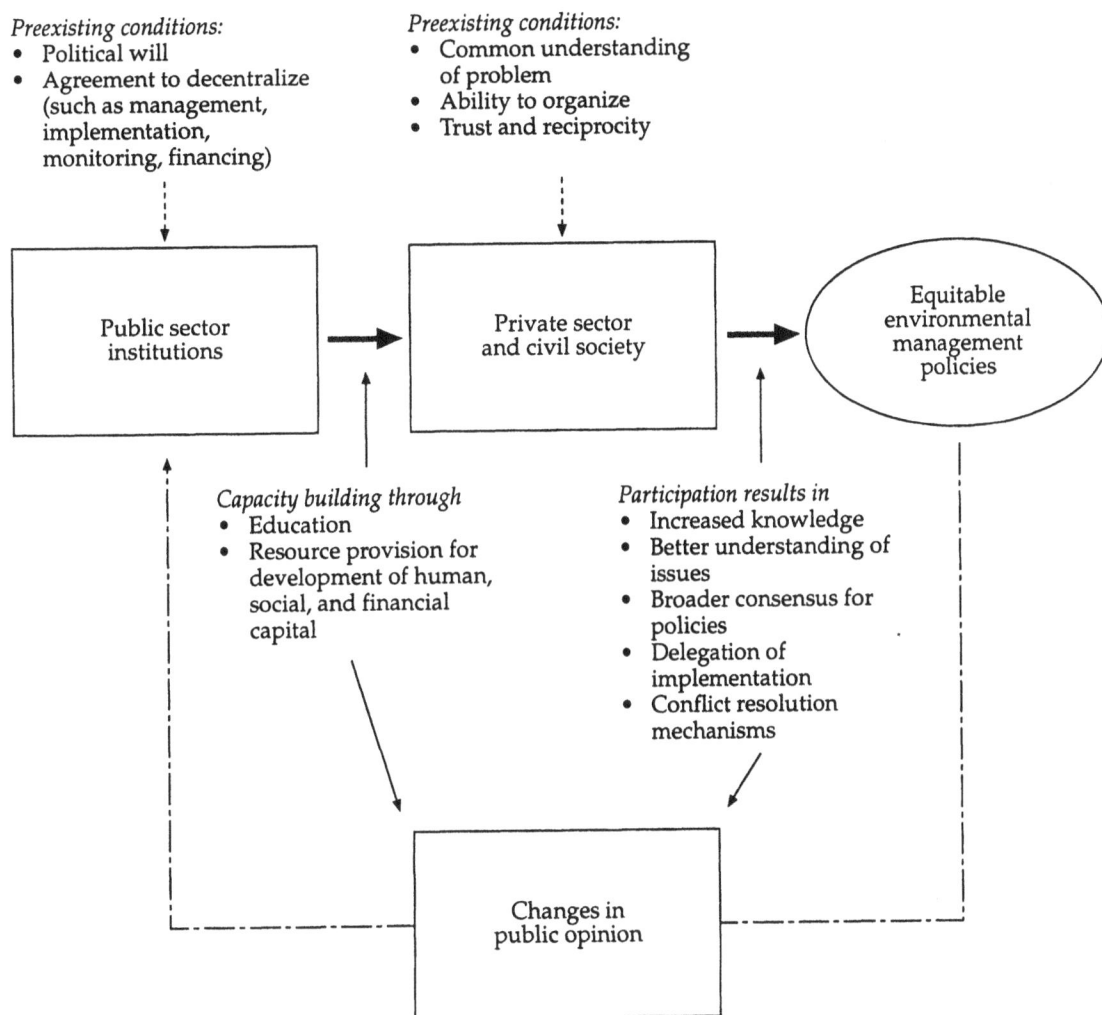

Preexisting conditions:
- Political will
- Agreement to decentralize (such as management, implementation, monitoring, financing)

Preexisting conditions:
- Common understanding of problem
- Ability to organize
- Trust and reciprocity

```
┌─────────────────┐      ┌─────────────────┐          ⬭ Equitable
│ Public sector   │─────▶│ Private sector  │─────▶   environmental
│ institutions    │      │ and civil society│          management
│                 │      │                 │          policies
└─────────────────┘      └─────────────────┘
```

Capacity building through
- Education
- Resource provision for development of human, social, and financial capital

Participation results in
- Increased knowledge
- Better understanding of issues
- Broader consensus for policies
- Delegation of implementation
- Conflict resolution mechanisms

```
┌─────────────────┐
│ Changes in      │
│ public opinion  │
└─────────────────┘
```

Source: Authors.

Government institutions have an important role to play in supporting local participation. After decades of top-down policies, local people have become passive and expect to be excluded from participation in designing solutions to development problems. Changing these attitudes takes time and requires active support by people in government institutions.

Community groups and NGOs can help local citizens become more active in the development process by facilitating capacity building through education and resource provision. These groups often excel in their ability to reach the rural poor in remote areas; promote local participation; and foster innovation, particularly in the use of low-cost technologies. However, they often have weak financial bases and administrative structures and limited technical capacities. Therefore, they frequently require strengthening through financial and technical assistance and management training.

Human and social capital must also be strengthened. All actors must have the social skills to collaborate in situations of nonadversarial decisionmaking, and training is needed to develop such skills. The most important effect of improved information and environmental education is to change individuals' behavior. The attitudes of government agency staff often impede participation by local groups. For example, forestry departments may see their mission as protecting trees from people. Similarly, wildlife conservation agencies may see local communities and game poachers as having the same intentions for natural resource use: exploitation. Countries should give high priority to changing these attitudes by increasing the organizational importance of units and bringing in staff with backgrounds in the social sciences who can assist in the move toward participatory approaches.

The Fruits of Participation

Active local involvement yields many benefits. Foremost, it results in more equitable policies and improves the likelihood that projects and programs will succeed. People's views about the environment strongly influence their management of it. Thus local communities will only support environmental programs and projects if they reflect local beliefs, values, and ideology and use the community.

Local involvement will also give policymakers a better and broader understanding of issues and give them access to new sources of local knowledge and expertise. Furthermore, it will increase the likelihood of greater consensus about policies, and therefore give more people incentives to become involved in implementation.

Many policies will require implementation at the national level, for example, taxes on resources, pollution fees, and so forth. When a population is more educated, aware of, and involved in environmental issues, public opinion is likely to support tougher policies that require people to change their habits and consumption patterns. Well-informed citizens can put more pressure on governments and on polluters and are more likely to accept the costs and inconveniences of environmental policies. Strong activism by local and national NGOs, lobbying groups, and the media contributes to the voicing of public opinion on these issues. These groups can also press for more accommodating policies toward public participation at all levels.

The experience of the National Irrigation Authority in the Philippines illustrates effective community-government interaction. The early involvement of community groups in the planning and construction of channels and drains has brought about better maintenance of irrigation works and improved water supply to farmers, resulting in higher agricultural yields. In addition, users have also been more willing to pay for the authority's services.

If provisions for true participation have been made, the resolution of conflicts, which are often inherent in environmental decisionmaking, will be easier. When mechanisms for conflict resolution exist and the community's voice can be heard, people may be less likely to overuse natural resources out of fear of losing access to them when large infrastructure investments in dams, irrigation facilities, roads, and ports are planned. Listening to public opinion and local NGOs and consulting with them at an early stage in the development of a project or policy is a good way to avoid conflicts during implementation phases. When this does not occur, community opposition can gather momentum and delay projects or stop them entirely.

Finally, a note of caution is necessary. The decentralization of decisionmaking can easily strengthen the power of local elites, who may use this to their individual advantage and not to the benefit of the community at large. Thus policies should adopt a balanced approach through accountability and transparency to offset such outcomes.

Conclusion

When implementing change, governments must make the best use of their scarce administrative resources. This requires improved information and analysis to set priorities and design effective policies; responsive and effective institutions suited to the administrative traditions of the particular location; and greater local participation in policymaking, monitoring, and enforcement.

Policymakers need to have access to and to build upon information and knowledge generated both in a range of scientific disciplines as well as in local and indigenous communities. Public sector institutions face the challenges of mainstreaming environmental considerations and coordinating policymaking and implementation across bureaucratic borders. They should also ensure that decisions are made with as much broad consensus building efforts as possible. Such efforts can make implementation more effective. An involved civil society will ensure more equitable environmental management policies and more effective implementation of those policies.

References

Wheeler, David, and Shakeb Afsah. 1996. *Going Public with Polluters in Indonesia: BAPEDAL's PROPER-PROKASH Program.* Washington, D.C.: International Executive Reports.

World Bank. 1992. *World Development Report 1992.* New York: Oxford University Press.

_____. 1996. *The World Bank Participation Source Book.* Washington, D.C.

Other Recommended Readings

Economic Commission for Latin America and the Caribbean (ECLAC). 1991. *Sustainable Development: Changing Production Patterns, Social Equity, and the Environment.* Santiago, Chile: United Nations and ECLAC.

Munasinghe, Mohan. 1993. *Environmental Economics and Sustainable Development.* Environment Paper no. 3. Washington, D.C.: World Bank.

Thomas, Vinod, Nalin Kishor, and Tamara Belt. 1997. "Embracing the Power of Knowledge for Sustainable Development." Background working paper for the *World Development Report 1998.* World Bank, Washington, D.C.

United Nations Conference on Environment and Development. 1992. *Agenda 21.* New York: United Nations Publications.

World Bank. 1997. *Five Years after Rio, Innovations in Environmental Policy.* Washington, D.C.

_____. 1997. *World Development Report 1997.* New York: Oxford University Press.

World Resources Institute. 1995. *Policy Hits the Ground: Participation and Equity in Environmental Policymaking.* New York: Oxford University Press.

6

Poverty, Income Distribution, and the Environment

Degraded environments can accelerate the process of impoverishment because the poor depend directly on natural resources for their food, energy, water, and income. When grasslands are degraded, livestock suffer and income is lost; when woodlands and forests are cleared, fuelwood becomes scarce and energy generation capacity is reduced; and when soils are eroded, crop productivity is reduced and income and food sources are lost. This chapter considers the links between poverty and the environment, the effects of income distribution on economic growth, the geographic location of the poor, and some policy responses that address these issues.

Links between Poverty and the Environment: The Mainstream View

People living in poverty face enormous difficulties in responding to rapid environmental change, especially if they lack a traditional knowledge base about nature and its uses. The mainstream view on the links between poverty and environmental resource degradation is that usually the planning time horizon of the poor is short and that they have few options available to them. The circumstances of the poor are compounded by poor health and illiteracy, which further reduce their ability to cope and survive. What remains is often two strategies of action. First, they can attempt to supplement their scarce assets by intensifying their use of open-access resources, which in turn may result in further resource depletion and environmental degradation. Second, they can migrate to an urban area, which would impose different pressures on natural resources and affect the circumstances in which they earn their livelihood in different ways from rural areas. Which course of action the poor take depends on the immediate options available, cultural and institutional factors, and local and national government policies.

Nevertheless, this relationship between poverty and the environment does not imply that poverty is a direct cause of environmental degradation. Rather, poverty should be seen as a disabling factor that reduces peoples' ability to allocate resources effectively and to respond to changes in the external environment appropriately.

Often poverty is exacerbated by rapid population growth, which in itself can exert negative effects on the environment. For example, in Bangladesh population growth is leading to reductions in average farm size, which is resulting in lower agricultural productivity and increased poverty. As poverty increases, the population's ability to escape environmental degradation is reduced even further. However, population growth is not necessarily a negative factor for the environment, in that it can strengthen communities and lead to improved use of resources through specialization and improved markets. A practical example of this is illustrated by a widely cited longitudinal study conducted in the Machakos District of Kenya (Tiffin, Mortimore, and Fichuki 1993), which shows that even when the population grew, no corresponding environmental degradation occurred. This was because land tenure was secure, credit was available, resources were properly priced, and marketing support and infrastructure were available for agricultural and other economic activities.

As figure 6.1 shows, a negative cycle does seem to exist between poverty, population growth, and environmental degradation.[1] However, many of the negative links between poverty and the environment can

---

Based on presentations by T. Banuri, J. Moyo, and N. Myers.

1. Empirically testing the causative characteristics of the links between poverty (as measured by per capita income) and environmental degradation is not possible, because reliable, comparable environmental indicators are

Figure 6.1.   Breaking the Cycle of Poverty-Environment-Population Growth

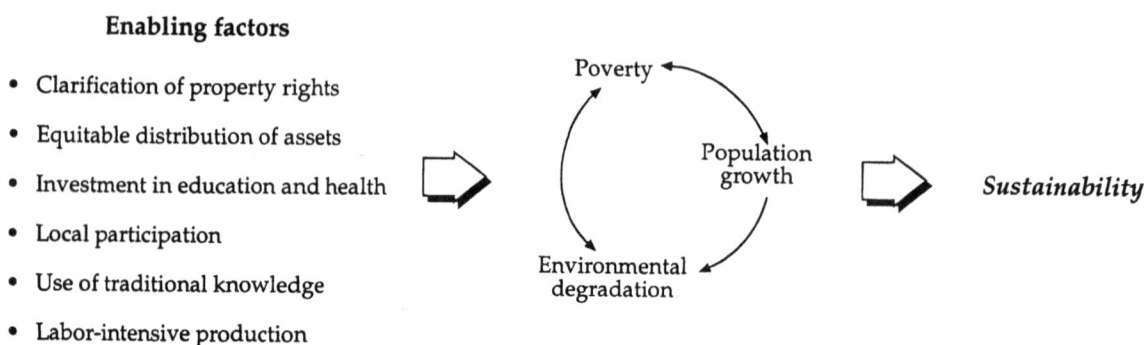

Enabling factors

- Clarification of property rights

- Equitable distribution of assets

- Investment in education and health

- Local participation

- Use of traditional knowledge

- Labor-intensive production

Poverty

Population growth

Environmental degradation

Sustainability

Source: Authors.

be broken if certain enabling factors are put in place, such as clarifying property rights; distributing income and assets more equitably; investing in education and health; promoting broadly based participation in economic activities by affected populations, for instance, women; and encouraging development based on the use of traditional knowledge and the intensive use of labor in production. These factors enable people to use resources more effectively. For instance, if people are better educated and encouraged to use their traditional knowledge, they will be able to become involved in productive economic activities, or if people have secure land tenure they will be more inclined to use sustainable cultivation and/or extraction methods, and not "mine" (deplete) resources and relocate when they are exhausted.

The existence of poverty does not mean that environmental degradation will necessarily follow. It also does not imply that poor people are responsible for the bulk of environmental degradation. Rather, it is the accumulation of wealth and the consumption patterns that follow that can be a major cause of environmental degradation(see chapter 7).

Income Distribution and Growth in the Developing World

Income distribution and growth can play an important role in environmental degradation. Table 6.1 presents Gini indexes for low-income countries in various parts of the world. The Gini index is a measure of inequality. The closer the index is to 100, the higher the level of inequality. Recent trends in the figures for Southeast Asia show that rapid economic growth was accompanied by substantial reductions in poverty, and inequity is not as great as in other developing regions, such as Latin America and the Caribbean, the Middle East and North Africa, and Sub-Saharan Africa. Economists have argued that this has been one of the reasons behind the economic growth in Southeast Asia: more equitable distribution of income leads to more efficient allocation of resources and widens the base for increased consumption and investment (for a discussion see World Bank 1993).

One example of the negative effects of a skewed distribution of income and assets is land tenure. In places with a high concentration of land ownership, as in Brazil and Colombia, production patterns tend to be capital intensive with low labor inputs, such as cattle ranching. This further diminishes the access of the poor to natural resources and exacerbates their condition.

not available. In addition, data about the extent to which gross domestic product is derived from resource-based activities, for instance, forestry and fisheries, are not available.

Table 6.1. *Gini Indexes, Selected Countries and Years*

Region, country, and survey year	Gini index
Africa	
Egypt, 1991	32.0
Kenya, 1992	57.5
Zambia, 1993	56.8
Zimbabwe, 1990	56.8
Asia	
Bangladesh, 1992	28.3
China, 1995	41.5
Malaysia, 1989	48.4
Thailand, 1992	46.2
Latin America	
Brazil, 1989	63.4
Colombia, 1991	57.3
Peru, 1994	44.9
Venezuela, 1990	53.8
Europe	
Bulgaria, 1992	30.8
Poland, 1992	27.2

Source: World Bank (1997, pp. 54–57).

The Geographic Location of the Poor

The link between poverty and environmental degradation can be further examined by analyzing where the poor are located. A large part of the world's poor live in the following three broad kinds of areas, the bulk of which are marginalized regions:

- Rural areas where agriculture is difficult because of poor soils or other biophysical characteristics, for example, sloping land and flooding and inundation
- Areas where the land's potential productivity is substantial, but the ability of the poor to use this effectively is diminished because of their reduced access to such resources as credit, land rights, and technology inputs
- Peri-urban areas where the poor are mostly confined to unhealthy and unsafe environments, for instance, open spaces along roadsides, river banks, steep slopes, flood plains, airport buffers, aquifers, and wetlands.

According to a study by Leonard (1987), the number of poor people that live in unstable environments globally is enormous. Of the 700 million poor, 100 million live in peripheral urban areas, which in turn are often areas of high risk because of the danger of landslides and floods and the lack of sanitation and infrastructure. An estimated 250 million poor live in areas where agriculture could be intensified by applying fertilizers and using modern technology, and any fragility in the system could be substituted with chemical inputs. Finally, close to 350 million poor people live in areas where such substitution is either more difficult or infeasible because of the climatic and soil conditions.

Environmental Degradation and Economic Growth

The process of growth and increasing economic production invariably leads to greater resource use. This can be destructive to the environment in different ways. In the main, during the initial stages of growth, environmental pressure is primarily exerted on the "green" areas, that is, in agriculture, forestry, and fisheries, and in mining, where renewable or nonrenewable resources are extracted. Problems with air pollution, for example, indoor pollution from stoves, and with toxic waste, for instance, dumping of obsolete pesticides, may also arise. As development progresses, increased pressures are exerted on the "brown" areas, including air and water pollution and the accumulation of waste products. At high-income levels, countries have more resources with which to address pollution problems, and certain areas of the environment exhibit clear improvements through investments in clean technologies, more efficient production techniques, and improved infrastructure, particularly water supply and sanitation. Because of the different types of environmental problems affecting the poor, targeted policies that mitigate negative effects on the green sector are necessary.

The Policy Response to Poverty and the Environment

The practical policy response to poverty should first aim at raising agricultural productivity in the most potentially productive areas, thereby improving the well-being of some of the most impoverished poor and reducing the pressure exerted on marginal lands. In marginal areas with poor soil, a range of different measures could improve agricultural productivity, such as traditional farming techniques, labor-intensive techniques, integrated pest management, and modern technology inputs. However, the productive capacity of each land area has limits that cannot be exceeded even with large capital inputs. In those areas where the potential productivity is naturally relatively high, technological inputs would have a major role to play in alleviating poverty. After this is achieved, policy should be directed toward second-generation issues, such as marketing and distribution channels for agricultural products that would further boost the incomes of poor farmers.

There is also a possibility for the poor to produce their own food in peri-urban areas by encouraging urban agriculture. Such production employs underutilized urban land efficiently; increases the food supply in urban areas, thereby helping to alleviate poverty; and may offset some of the dependence and environmental pressure on rural agriculture (United Nations Development Programme 1996).

In all three areas the policy mix must include incentive schemes that consist of increased investment, improved physical infrastructure, credit, and extension information. More broadly, institution building is needed, such as establishing or reinforcing property rights through land and resource tenure. Such schemes are more long term and often involve difficult political decisions. Therefore, when setting priorities, infrastructure, investment, and extension activities are more easily implemented, and tougher policies, such as those dealing with property rights, may best be dealt with in the medium term.

Efforts to meet the challenge of reducing poverty have increasingly moved toward a decentralized approach, whereby households, farms, communities, and local and national governments are involved in policy design and implementation (see chapter 5). These concerted efforts must be at the forefront of policymaking.

Links between Poverty and the Environment: An Alternative View

Other investigators argue that the mainstream view focuses on the immediate causes rather than on the key driving forces dictating the resource users' behavior. Jodha (1998) states that widespread evidence indicates that many villagers who are currently facing severe environmental degradation were actually poorer in the past, yet they consciously prevented environmental degradation. Furthermore, in many areas of the world richer groups contribute more to resource degradation that the poor. Jodha believes that those who are part of the mainstream view, that is, those who think that poverty and scarcity cause desperation, which in turn promotes overextraction of natural resources, leading to greater degradation and hence even greater scarcity and poverty, are making three unjustified assumptions as follows:

- That the overextraction of natural resources is the only or preferred means of sustenance that poor people know
- That the poor are ignorant of both the limitations of their environmental resources and the consequences of their extractive practices
- That the poor have little stake in the health and productivity of their natural resources.

Rather, says Jodha, many poor communities have over time developed methods of sustenance based on the limitations and potential of their local natural resource base, and some evidence exists to indicate that this traditional knowledge base survives and grows even when communities have been dislocated and resettled. The key features of their adaptations were as follows:

- A high dependence on the local natural resource base, leading to an explicit realization of the strong links between their sustenance and the protection and productivity of this natural resource base.
- The frequent isolation of poor communities and their closeness to their natural resources leads to a strong understanding of the importance, limitations, and usefulness of natural resources. The communities therefore develop folk technologies to protect and regenerate the resources while making use of them. They also create a series of locally enforceable regulatory measures to monitor the intensity of resource use, for instance, social sanctions.

By adopting such practices and behavior, poor communities develop a traditional system of natural resource management that helps them avoid the poverty-environmental resource degradation link. However, these arrangements break down with the advent of outside advisers who design and implement external interventions at the grassroots level without sufficient understanding of local realities and communities' concerns, capabilities, and knowledge (Jodha 1998). Increased physical, administrative, and market integration of what used to be less accessible areas with the mainstream view reduced the crucial dependence of local communities on their natural resource base. While these interventions brought with them some benefits, they also created some perverse incentives that eventually led to the disintegration of communities' stakes in natural resources and the marginalization of the local knowledge system and institutional arrangements that helped to protect the natural resource base.

Given the ineffectiveness of interventions directed to preventing human-induced degradation of the environment, a temptation is to go back to the traditional way of living; however, traditional measures have suffered so much transformation that their revival would likely be impossible. Instead, we should search for functional substitutes that would suit today's circumstances. Table 6.2 lists possible ways to revive traditional methods of natural resource base management, along with the constraints. Many of these suggested possibilities are supported by evidence from successful experiences, such as user group forestry in Nepal, joint forest management in parts of India, and several other initiatives run by nongovernmental organizations.

Policymakers ought to consider these points before implementing projects and advising poor communities on how they should manage their resources. The mainstream view linking poverty to natural resource degradation has some fairly convincing arguments on its side; however, policymakers should keep alternative views in mind, because many are relevant to the issue of poverty-environmental resource degradation links. The key point is that incorporating alternative views within mainstream practices may generate the best outcomes.

Conclusion

The circular link between poverty, environmental degradation, and poverty is complex and difficult to break. Poverty leads to unsustainable use of resources, because the poor have few immediate alternative options open to them in the short run. Because they depend on natural resources for their livelihood, the degradation of these resources exacerbates their condition.

Table 6.2. Possibilities for and Constraints to Reviving Traditional Resource Use Systems

Community stake in local natural resources	Local control over local natural resources	Recognition and use of resource users' perspectives and traditional knowledge systems
Constraints		
• Formal legal, administrative, and fiscal controls and restrictions creating perverse incentives; reactive mode of community behavior as individuals	• State's resistance to self-disempowerment through passing decisionmaking power to local communities	• Top-down interventions with a mix of arrogance, ignorance, and insensitivity toward local traditional systems
• Highly depleted status of the natural resource base, preventing hope and incentive to have a stake in it	• Faction-ridden, rural communities driven by diverse signals and concerns	• Focus on forms of traditional practices rather than their rationale for use in the current context
• More heterogeneous communities with diverging individual views, rather than group views on community resources	• NGOs as key change-facilitating agents, often governed by own perspectives	• Rapid disappearance of indigenous knowledge
Possible remediation		
• Genuine local autonomy for local resource management; legal framework and support system for natural resource user groups	• Genuine decentralization of decisionmaking powers and resources to communities	• Promotion of bottom-up approaches to resource management strategies, using participatory methods and NGO help
• Resource protection, investment, and use of new technologies for regeneration and high productivity of the natural resource base	• Rebuilding social capital using NGOs; focus on diversified, high-value products from rehabilitated natural resource base	• Focused efforts to identify present-day functional substitutes of traditional measures for resource management
• Collective stake through planned diversification and shareholding system in natural resource development and gains	• Required changes in NGO approaches by introspection; involving small local groups	• Research and development to incorporate rationale of traditional knowledge systems

NGO Nongovernmental organization.
Source: Adapted from Jodha (1998, p. 3).

Because poverty is a disabling factor rather than an underlying cause of environmental degradation, other compounding issues must be taken into account, such as population growth, poor health, illiteracy, and marginalization. Enabling factors do exist that can help break the destructive reinforcing relationship of poverty-population growth-environmental degradation. Some of the key enabling factors are improved access to resources, clarified property rights, growth driven by labor-intensive production, education, and the integration of traditional knowledge in development.

The fact that a significant number of the world's poorest people live in environments that are biophysically fragile poses special challenges to policymakers. Policy responses should focus on strengthening the enabling factors. Human capital is the most vital resource an economy has. Reducing poverty, decreasing the gap between the rich and the poor, and improving resource use can have a tremendous impact in fortifying this resource.

An alternative view of looking at the links between poverty and the environment acknowledges that if poor communities revert to traditional systems of natural resource management, they can manage their environment efficiently, or even improve it, despite being poor.

References

Jodha, N. S. 1998. *Poverty-Environmental Resource Degradation Links: Questioning the Basic Premises*. Issues in Mountain Development no. 98/1. Kathmandu, Nepal: International Centre for Integrated Mountain Development.

Leonard, H. J. 1987. *Natural Resources and Economic Development in Central America: A Regional Environmental Profile*. New Brunswick, New Jersey: Transaction Books.

Tiffin, M., M. Mortimore, and F. N. Fichuki. 1993. *More People, Less Erosion: Environmental Recovery in Kenya*. New York: J. Wiley and Sons.

United Nations Development Programme. 1996. *Urban Agriculture, Food, Jobs, and Sustainable Cities*. New York.

World Bank. 1993. *The East Asian Miracle*. New York: Oxford University Press.

_____. 1997. *World Development Indicators*. Washington, D.C.

Other Recommended Readings

Boserup, E. 1965. *The Conditions of Agricultural Growth: The Economics of Agrarian Change under Population Pressure*. New York: Aldine.

Dasgupta, P. 1995. *An Inquiry into Well-Being and Destitution*. Oxford, U.K.: Clarendon Press.

Hanna, S., and M. Munasinghe. 1995. *Property Rights and the Environment, Social, and Ecological Issues*. Washington, D.C.: Beijer International Institute of Ecological Economics and World Bank.

Lopez, R. 1997. "Where Development Can or Cannot Go: The Role of Poverty-Environment Linkages." Paper presented at the Annual World Bank Conference on Development Economics, April 30–May 1, Washington, D.C.

Moser, Caroline. 1997. *Confronting Crisis: A Summary of Household Responses to Poverty and Vulnerability in Four Poor Urban Communities*. Washington, D.C.: World Bank.

Pearce, D. W., and J. J. Warford. 1993. *World Without End*. New York: Oxford University Press.

World Bank. 1991. *World Development Report 1991*. New York: Oxford University Press.

7

Population, Natural Resources, and the Environment

The world's population has increased rapidly during the past two centuries: between 1800 and 1930 it doubled from 1 to 2 billion people, but took only 45 more years to double again to 4 billion by 1975. By 2025 the world's population is projected to total about 8.3 billion people, and by 2050 is estimated to be 10 billion, with the bulk of growth occurring in developing countries. The environmental effects of population growth appear to be closely related to increases in air and water pollution, municipal and industrial wastes, deforestation, and loss of biodiversity. This implies that a comprehensive population policy is important for long-term solutions to environmental problems.

Trends in Population Growth

In industrial countries, high birthrates accompanied rapid economic growth during the industrial revolution, mainly because of improved public health. As countries became more prosperous, both death and birthrates decreased, resulting in low population growth rates. Today, most of the developing world is characterized by high birthrates for much the same reasons as in the industrial countries in the past. At the same time, death rates have fallen dramatically, mainly because of improvements in health care, education, and sanitation. Even though birthrates have declined substantially in many developing countries during the past 25 years, they still remain high, mainly for the following reasons:

- Wherever agriculture is an important activity for poor households, they have an incentive to invest in children to serve as farm labor and assist with household tasks, such as fuelwood and water collection and childcare.
- When large families provide social security through the extended family, investing in children becomes a way of ensuring care in old age.
- Lack of knowledge about family planning.

Figure 7.1 shows projections for world population under different fertility trends, and figure 7.2 shows population growth projections for different regions of the world.

Three global demographic trends can be identified. The first trend is that fertility rates have been declining since the 1960s, and estimates indicate that current average fertility worldwide is three children per woman. Demographic stability is most closely linked to the point at which a nation's fertility rate drops to the replacement level of about two children per woman. As figure 7.1 indicates, projections show that on a global level, replacement fertility levels will be reached by 2060.

The second important world demographic trend is the aging of the world's population. Average life expectancy is increasing because of improved nutrition and health care.

The third salient trend is that a large proportion of the world's population is living in urban areas (figure 7.3). By 2030 urban populations will be twice the size of rural populations. The population in cities in developing countries will have grown by 160 percent by 2030, whereas rural populations will have grown by only 10 percent. By 2000, 21 cities will have more than 10 million inhabitants, with most of these cities being in developing countries.

Based on presentations by J. W. Warford and W. A. Ward.

Figure 7.1. *World Population Projections under Different Fertility Trends, 1985–2160*

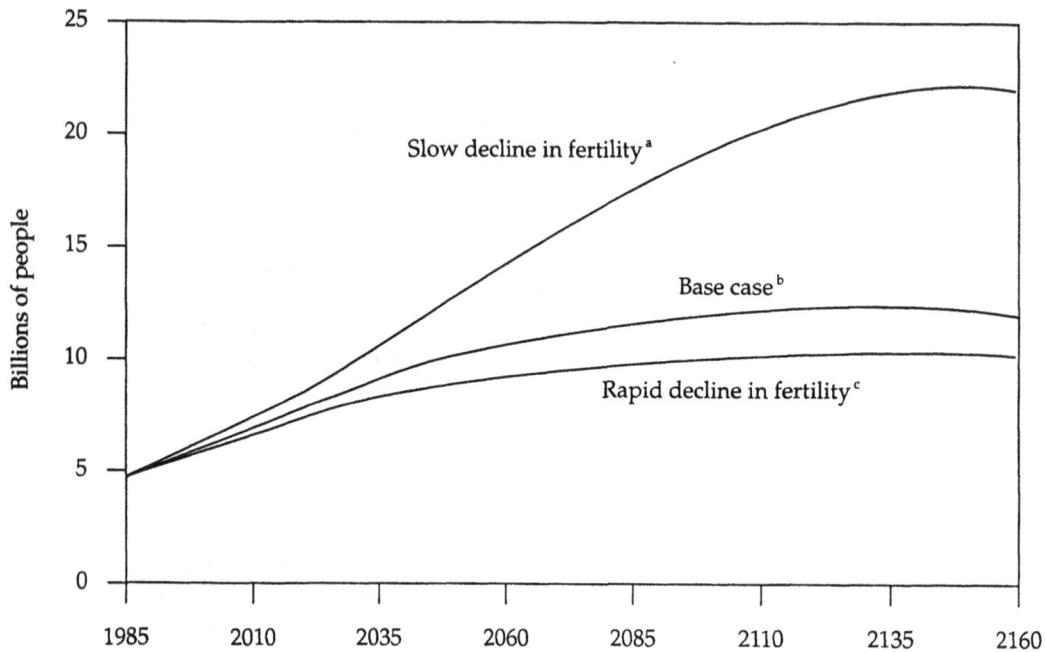

a. Transition toward lower fertility—triggered when life expectancy reaches 53 years—begins after 2020 in most low-income countries. For countries in transition, declines are half the rate for the base case.

b. Countries with high and nondeclining fertility levels begin the transition toward lower fertility by year 2005 and undergo a substantial decline—by more than half in many cases—over the next 40 years. All countries reach replacement fertility levels by 2060.

c. Countries not yet in transition toward lower fertility begin the transition immediately. For countries already in transition, total fertility declines at twice the rate for the base case.

Source: World Bank (1992, p. 26).

The Links between Population and Environment

Rapid population growth and imbalances in the distribution of population in relation to natural resources can increase environmental degradation and undermine sustainable development. This is particularly evident in the case of the following problems:

- *Soil erosion and desertification,* which are often brought on by demographic pressures among the poorest groups, population migration into marginal areas, and environmental refugees
- *Deforestation and loss of biodiversity* resulting from inappropriate cultivation techniques, demand for fuelwood, and conversion of forests in upland areas to other uses
- *Misuse and pollution of freshwater resources* in both rural and urban areas, caused mainly by the concentration of the population in and around congested towns and cities
- *Production of greenhouse gases,* which is linked with changing land use, agricultural practices— particularly slash and burn practices—and increased industrial and urban pollution
- *Pollution in coastal areas,* especially where urban populations are growing rapidly and critical resources are being depleted at an accelerated rate.

Figure 7.4 illustrates some of the intermediate effects that increasing population density might have on different sectors of the economy. For example, in agriculture, existing resources might be used more intensively, resulting in shorter fallow periods and lower soil productivity. Population pressure may also force colonization in areas of unused resources, for instance, "frontier" resources such as forests and

Figure 7.2. *Actual and Projected Population Growth Rates by Region, 1850–2025*

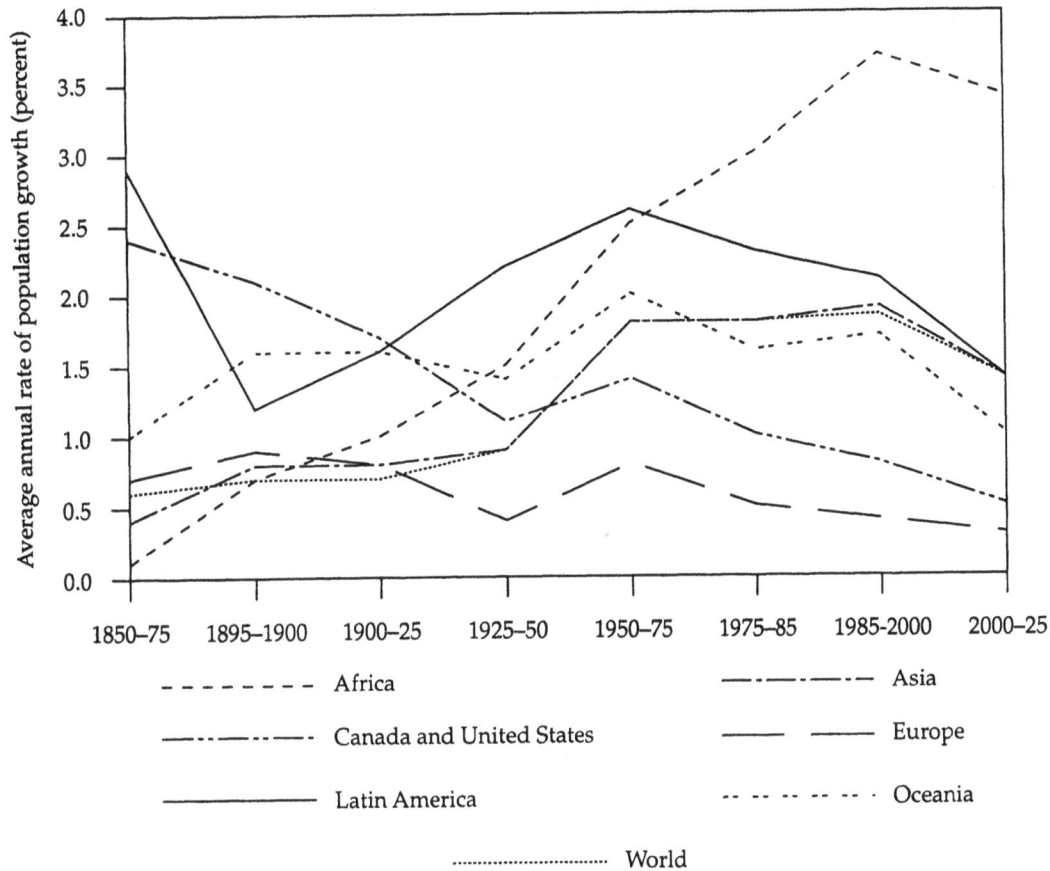

Source: Pearce and Warford (1993, p. 153).

hillsides. Because older agricultural practices may not be appropriate for the newly cleared land, soil erosion and low soil productivity may follow, resulting in lower yields. The poverty that this induces may itself lead to more marginal lands being converted to farming, thereby accelerating the cycle of population, poverty, and environmental degradation (see chapter 6 for more details).

Population growth need not necessarily lead to increased pressure on the environment. The impact could also be positive. Boserup (1965) asserts that as population grows, land and other natural resources become scarcer relative to labor, and access to markets improves. Thus population growth may encourage farmers to intensify agriculture by adopting technological change, and may even be the main stimulus for increased productivity.

The positive influence that population growth may have on agricultural productivity is caused by shorter fallow periods and increased farming intensity. Although this reduces soil productivity, farmers may react by introducing technological change that can counteract declines in soil productivity. The relative speed with which technology evolves compared with the rate of decline in soil productivity and the increase in population growth determines the rate of change in agricultural productivity. Note, however, that technology itself can have significant negative environmental effects, for example, the effects of fertilizer runoff on water systems, of pesticides on human and ecosystem health, and of monocultural cropping on the resilience of ecosystems to shock and stress. For these reasons, policy must continue to be directed toward improving technology and its application and reducing the rate of population growth.

Figure 7.3. *Actual and Projected Rural and Urban Populations by Region and Income, 1960–2025*

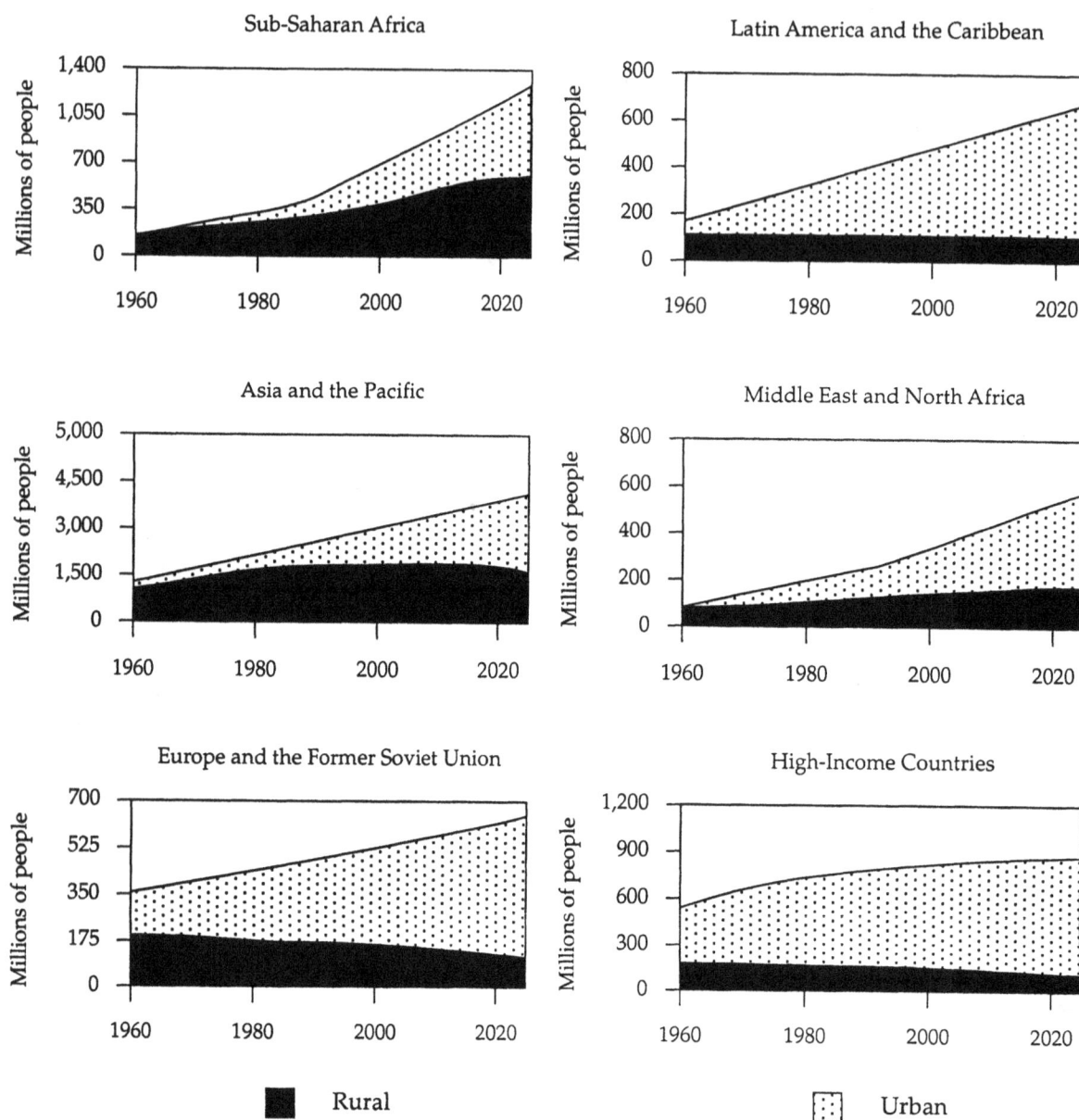

Rural

Urban

Source: World Bank (1992, p. 28).

In many cases, the evolution of more densely populated communities has led to increased poverty and environmental destruction in developing countries. However, many factors other than population growth also result in increased agricultural activity in ecologically unsuitable areas, such as research and development, investment, prices, and land tenure. If these are unfavorable, population growth will not have a positive influence on economic development.

Population and Consumption Patterns

Increasing population implies increased consumption of natural resources. The countries of the Organisation for Economic Co-operation and Development (OECD) place huge demands on the world's

Figure 7.4.   Links among Population, the Environment, and Poverty

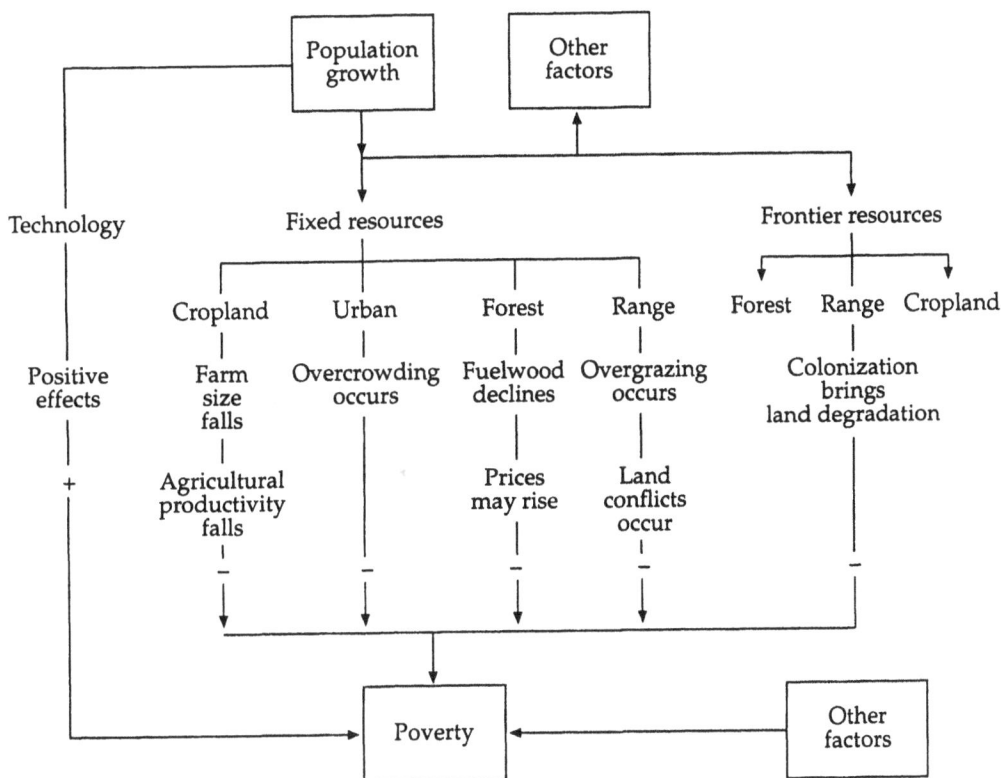

Source: Pearce and Warford (1993, p. 150).

resources and are responsible for a large share of the world's pollution burden. For example, the United States consumes 45 to 55 barrels of oil per capita per year, whereas Bangladesh consumes only 3 barrels per capita per year. On a per capita basis, the share of consumption of the largest OECD economies is often several times the world average (table 7.1). Despite having only a quarter of the world's population, the industrial nations consume 75 percent of all energy produced, 79 percent of all commercial fuels, 85 percent of all wood products, and 72 percent of all steel products (Shaw 1992, p. 119).

The combined population of the OECD countries represents only 16 percent of the world's population, yet in 1989 the OECD countries released approximately 40 percent of global sulfur dioxide emissions and 54 percent of nitrogen oxide emissions, the primary sources of acid precipitation. They accounted for 38 percent of the potential global warming impact on the atmosphere from emissions of greenhouse gases. Likewise, industrial countries generate more than three-quarters of all municipal, industrial, and nuclear wastes.

Despite some improvements, air and water pollution and disposal of large quantities of waste remain serious problems in virtually all OECD countries. Industrial residues—acidic materials, heavy metals, and toxic chemicals—degrade soils, damage plants, and endanger food supplies. On a per capita basis, the OECD countries are overwhelmingly the world's major polluters, both within their own borders and in their contribution to global environment degradation.

The combined effects of population growth, access to polluting technologies, and higher consumption levels will increase global waste from around 2.5 billion metric tons in 1985 to more than 4.5 billion metric tons by 2025. In 1985 the developing nations contributed 25 percent of global waste, but if current consumption trends continue, they will probably contribute more than 50 percent by 2025 (Shaw 1992, p. 120).

Table 7.1. *Average Annual Resource Consumption Per Capita, Various Years*

Resource	Year of data	Canada	Germany	France	Italy	Japan	United Kingdom	United States	Average world consumption	Average for countries listed
Energy (exajoules)										
Total fossil fuels	1989	270.95	160.98	94.98	106.50	109.80	142.11	282.93	54.71	190.32
Solids	1989	44.65	74.41	14.48	10.01	26.96	47.94	80.15	18.71	53.13
Liquids	1989	127.06	57.75	60.24	69.35	67.51	56.97	127.21	22.48	90.27
Gas	1989	99.25	28.82	20.26	27.19	15.33	37.20	75.57	13.53	46.92
Metals (million metric tons)										
Crude steel	1989	529.72	563.08	312.77	486.70	757.64	304.00	441.44	153.20	489.09
Aluminum, refined	1990	15.66	17.83	12.77	11.32	19.55	7.89	17.24	3.39	15.94
Copper, refined	1990	6.95	13.29	8.46	8.24	12.76	5.52	8.54	2.04	9.54
Lead, refined	1990	3.44	5.79	4.51	4.48	3.38	5.25	5.13	1.05	4.71
Nickel, refined	1990	0.46	1.21	0.79	0.47	1.29	0.57	0.50	0.16	0.76
Tin, refined	1990	0.11	0.28	0.15	0.11	0.28	0.18	0.15	0.04	0.19
Zinc, slab	1990	4.75	6.85	5.03	4.69	6.59	3.29	3.95	1.32	4.93
Industrial materials (million metric tons)										
Cement	1983–85	239.86	502.67[b]	376.17	670.10	550.66	242.85	327.23	197.72[a]	416.06
Fertilizer	1989/90	82.67	58.39	108.67	31.52	15.74	41.22	75.21	27.63	58.18
Forest products										
Roundwood (million cubic meters)	1989	6.71	0.56	0.70	0.27	0.68	0.12	2.04	0.67	1.35
Paper and paperboard (million metric tons)	1989	236.09	181.62	148.17	116.00	221.84	168.15	306.71	44.39	229.61

a. World consumption assumed to be equal to world production.

b. Consumption in Federal Republic of German plus production in German Democratic Republic.

Note: Totals may not add because of independent rounding.

Source: World Resources Institute (1992, p. 18).

Nonrenewable Natural Resources

Higher incomes and living standards lead to increased consumption of nonrenewable resources per capita and thus exert more pressure on the environment. Table 7.2 shows the increase in energy consumption brought about by increases in population and higher living standards. While population growth has a significant impact on the volume of nonrenewable resources consumed, as indicated by the example of energy, rising incomes account for more of the world's growing consumption of energy than population growth.

Renewable Natural Resources

Population growth also affects the availability of renewable resources. Table 7.3 outlines broad estimates of changes in land use for the world's major countries and regions between 1850 and 1980. Increases in agricultural output were achieved mainly by expanding the area under cultivation. This expansion has been achieved at the cost of losses in forest land, wetlands, and grasslands. Figure 7.5 shows the relationship between forest coverage and population density based on cross-sectional data from 60 countries.

Table 7.2. Population Growth and Energy Consumption by Region, Selected Years

Region	Percentage of increased energy consumption due to increased		Energy consumption per capita (billions of joules)		
	Population	Living standards	1960	1984	1994
Africa	33	67	6	12	13
Asia	18	82	8	20	30
Europe	16	84	72	124	138
North America	51	49	—	—	—
Canada	—	—	164	286	329
United States	—	—	236	281	334
South America	37	63	16	28	35
World	46	54	38	55	58

— Not available.
Source: Adapted from Pearce and Warford (1993, p. 163); figures for 1960 and 1984 computed from United Nations Environment Programme (1987); figures for 1994 from United Nations (1996, table 3).

Table 7.3. Changes in Land Use by Selected Country and Region, 1850–1980
(percentage change in area)

Region	Forests	Grasslands	Cropland
China	-39	-3	+79
Europe	+4	+8	-4
Latin America	-19	-23	+677
North America	-3	-22	+309
South Asia	-43	-1	+196
Southeast Asia	-7	-25	+670
Former Soviet Union	-12	-1	+147
Tropical Africa	-20	+9	+288
All countries and regions	-15	-1	+179

Source: Pearce and Warford (1993, p. 165).

Figure 7.5.   *Relationship between Forest Coverage and Population Density in 60 Tropical Countries, 1980*

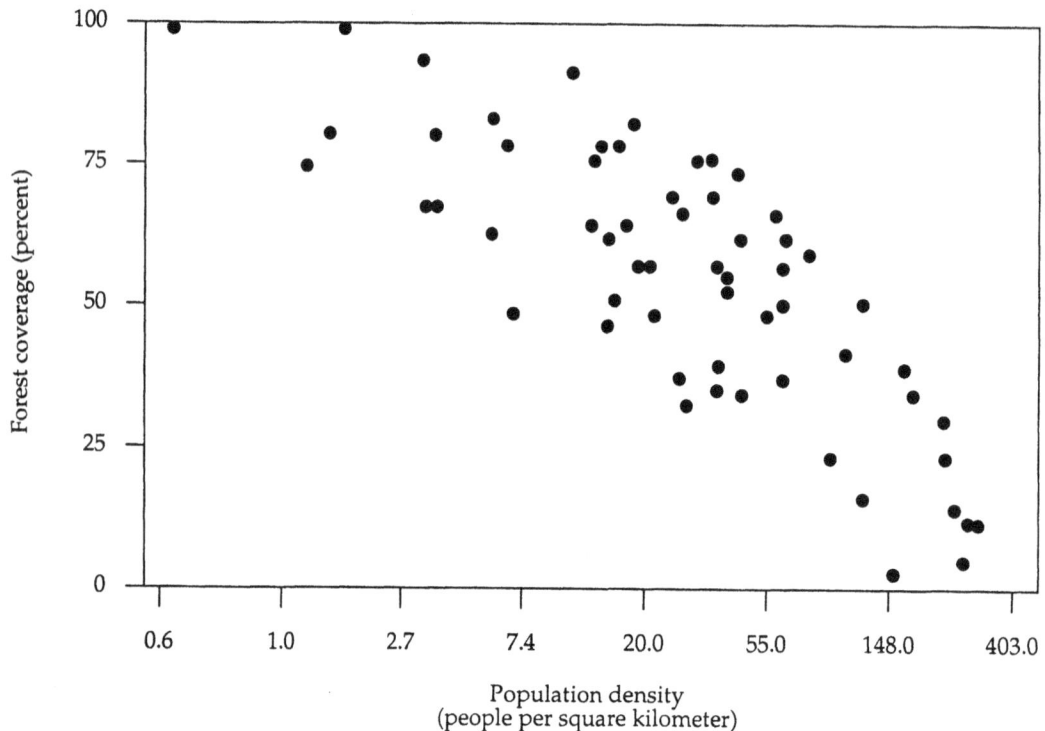

Source: Pearce and Warford (1993, p. 166).

This and similar studies indicate that population change can be an important proximate cause of deforestation. However, as noted earlier, many other factors are primary causes, such as land tenure, subsidies for deforestation, and economywide policies.

Population growth poses a considerable threat to biodiversity through its indirect effect on deforestation. Because most land suitable for crop production is now inhabited, population growth will lead to the destruction of forests and other sensitive areas, such as hillsides, semiarid regions, and coastal zones. Coastal zones are particularly important, because some 66 percent of the world's population live within 60 kilometers of a coastline (United Nations Environment Programme 1995, p. 771), and such zones are an important source of livelihoods and protein in the form of fishing. Coastal zones also have higher population growth rates than average because of migration from inland areas. This is particularly true in Africa, Asia, and South America.

Coastal areas possess unique ecosystems, such as mangrove swamps, eel grass beds, and coral reefs. These areas function as breeding grounds for many of the world's marine resources. However, with high and increasing population densities in coastal zones, these ecosystems are under threat from, for example, construction and pollution from domestic, agricultural, and industrial sources. In many areas mangrove forests have been cut down to give way for buildings or shrimp farms. The manmade structures lead to further deforestation, because they destroy the mangrove buffer. All these types of deterioration of coastal environments have a major effect on the production and availability of marine resources for human consumption.

Policy Recommendations

Considerable evidence suggests that population growth at its present rates threatens both the quality and quantity of natural resources, including the environment's capacity to absorb pollution and waste. Some argue that population growth may help increase gross national product per capita, which is true if a number of conditions exist, such as secure property rights, equitable land distribution, and appropriate technology. Nonetheless, increased gross national product implies increased per capita consumption.

In addition to mitigating the effects of population growth on the environment and natural resources, policy should address population growth itself. A number of elements constitute essential elements of such a policy, including the following:

- Improving literacy rates, especially for women.
- Empowering women as managers in environmental matters and family planning decisions.
- Having better knowledge for decisionmaking and collecting data on those aspects of demographic trends (for example, population size, growth rate, composition, and spatial distribution) that have the greatest impacts on the environment in ecologically endangered zones such as tropical forests, forested upland areas, smallholder agriculture in lowlands, arid areas used for grazing, coastal fishing areas, and urban slums.
- Encouraging involvement at the grassroots level and by nongovernmental organizations with respect to agricultural and rural development, forest preservation, maintenance of freshwater systems, health and nutrition, and safe motherhood.
- Reviewing family planning efforts in the context of macroeconomic and sectoral polices, particularly education and health. These types of basic investments are needed so that an enabling environment exists for women to become economically active.

Important factors that reduce the effectiveness of population policies are insufficient financing, problems of governance and implementation, and a lack of political will and trained personnel. In the past, donor influence has been substantial in initiating and financing population programs. These efforts have been important, but the volume of aid is not always an indication of its effectiveness. Even if a good official population policy existed, translating that policy into action would be difficult without a cadre of well-trained and committed personnel to monitor and evaluate family planning needs or to design and implement effective supply programs. Inadequate salaries, poor career prospects, and limited research and infrastructure (offices, computer facilities, and so on) are also important issues that influence access to such essential human resources.

Conclusion

Under certain circumstances population growth can have positive effects on economic growth and technological development. More frequently, however, high population growth leads to environmental degradation through settlements in sensitive ecosystems, increased demand on natural resources, and pollution. Patterns of migration and resulting population densities show an increasing trend toward urbanization, along with greater environmental problems.

A wide range of policies are needed in the education, health, and environmental sectors to reverse the current trends of high population growth and its accompanying effects on the environment. While the policies required to reduce population growth in the long run are clear, strong political will and commitment are needed on the part of developing countries to pursue these policies, as well as on the part of the industrial countries to assist financially and technically. Rich countries are consuming exceedingly more than poorer ones. Such a divergence raises the issue of equity. These countries should change their consumption patterns from overconsumption to a more appropriate one, and most important, this change must be accompanied by technology, capital (investment), and especially knowledge transfers.

References

Boserup, E. 1965. *The Conditions of Agricultural Growth*. London: Allen and Unwin.

Pearce, David W., and Jeremy W. Warford. 1993. *World Without End*. New York: Oxford University Press.

Shaw, R. Paul. 1992. "Population's Success Story, Environment's Nightmare." In *Green Globe Yearbook*. New York: Oxford University Press.

United Nations. 1996. *1994 Energy Statistics Yearbook*. New York: United Nations Publications.

United Nations Environment Programme. 1987. *Environmental Data Report*. Oxford, U.K.: Blackwell.

_____. 1995. *Global Biodiversity Assessment*. New York: Cambridge University Press.

World Bank. 1992. *World Development Report 1992*. New York: Oxford University Press.

World Resources Institute. 1992. *World Resources 1992–93*. New York: Oxford University Press.

Other Recommended Readings

Boserup, E. 1981. *Population and Technology*. Oxford, U.K.: Basil Blackwell.

Cleaver, Kevin M., and Gotz A. Schreiber. 1992. *The Population, Agriculture, and Environment Nexus in Sub-Saharan Africa*. Washington, D.C.: World Bank.

Dasgupta, P. 1992. "Population, Resources, and Poverty." *Ambio* 21(1): 95–101.

McMichael, A. J. 1993. *Planetary Overload*. Cambridge, U.K.: Cambridge University Press.

World Resources Institute. 1994. *World Resources 1994–95*. New York: Oxford University Press.

_____. 1996. *World Resources 1996–97*. New York: Oxford University Press.

8

Energy Consumption and the Environment

Unsustainable dependence on fossil fuels that contribute to greenhouse gas emissions is one of today's major global problems related to energy use. In addition, severe local and regional pollution problems caused by energy conversion processes also need to be addressed because of their adverse impact on human health and ecosystems. Solutions to these problems lie in choosing the right management options in the energy sector. The impetus behind radical policy changes will need to come from ethical imperatives for sustainable development.

Energy Use

Energy use affects the environment in different ways depending on the source, for instance, oil, coal, or biomass, and the efficiency of its use.

Environmental Impact

The environmental cost of energy use stems primarily from the damage caused by continued reliance on fossil fuels, and to a lesser extent on nuclear energy. Major effects resulting from the consumption of fossil fuels include the following:

- Local air pollution from lead, sulfur, and nitrous oxides, as well as from ozone in urban areas
- Regional air pollution, such as acid rain stemming from sulfur and nitrous oxides
- Global air pollution in the form of greenhouse gas emissions such as carbon dioxide and methane.

In developing countries, local pollution is the most urgent problem. However, regional pollution is growing, and the global implications of emissions from fossil fuels are escalating. This is most clearly manifested in the Framework Convention on Climate Change.

Energy sources other than fossil fuels also have environmental, social, or health impacts. For example, the use of biomass for indoor cooking causes respiratory diseases, the use of hydroelectric power has resulted in flooded croplands and displaced people, nuclear power has caused widespread radiation, and in some instances disposal of nuclear waste continues to be unsafe for human and ecological health.

The aforementioned effects are due mostly to energy consumption, but serious problems are also associated with the pollution and transport aspects of energy. A few examples are oil drilling in sensitive marine areas, oil spillage from tankers around the world, and the impact of uranium mining on the local environment. Most of the discussion in this chapter will focus on energy consumption, because that is the driving force behind these environmental problems. A decrease in the demand for fossil fuels would also induce a reduction in damage linked to production and transportation.

Global Consumption

During the past two centuries, energy consumption has, on average, increased by 2 percent per year globally, with some variations over time and across regions (Intergovernmental Panel on Climate Change,

---

Based on presentations by R. Ramani.

Working Group 2 1996). Energy use per capita is the highest in industrial countries, and so is air pollution per capita. For instance, carbon dioxide emissions per capita are 4 to 10 times higher in high-income countries than in low-income countries (World Bank 1997, pp. 110–113). In 1992 high-income countries were responsible for 48 percent of total emissions; however, carbon dioxide emissions per capita decreased from 1980 to 1992 (World Bank 1997, pp. 110–113). As table 8.1 shows, in 1994 per capita energy consumption in high-income countries was considerably higher than in low-income countries, in some cases 100 times as much.

The total consumption of commercial energy in developing countries is increasing rapidly, and projections indicate that in a couple of decades it will surpass the combined consumption levels of Organisation for Economic Co-operation and Development (OECD) countries and former Eastern bloc countries. Nevertheless, per capita energy use will still be considerably lower than in the OECD countries.

Energy Use by Sector

Figure 8.1 compares the use of commercial energy in the major sectors—electricity generation, industry, transport, and household—in developing and industrial countries.

Table 8.1. *Energy Consumption by Selected Regions and Economies, 1994*

Region and economy	Kilograms of oil equivalent per capita
Africa	
Kenya	110
Libya	2,499
Malawi	39
Mozambique	40
Asia	
Hong Kong, China*	2,185
India	248
Indonesia	366
Japan	3,856
Singapore*	8,103
Europe and the former Soviet Union	
Hungary	2,383
Italy*	2,707
Kyrgyz Republic	616
Poland*	2,401
Portugal	1,827
Russia	4,014
United Kingdom*	3,772
North and South America	
Argentina	1,504
Colombia	622
El Salvador	370
Trinidad and Tobago	5,436
United States*	7,819

* High-income economies.
Source: World Bank (1997).

Figure 8.1. Commercial Energy Consumption, 1988

Eight developing countries[a]   Industrial countries

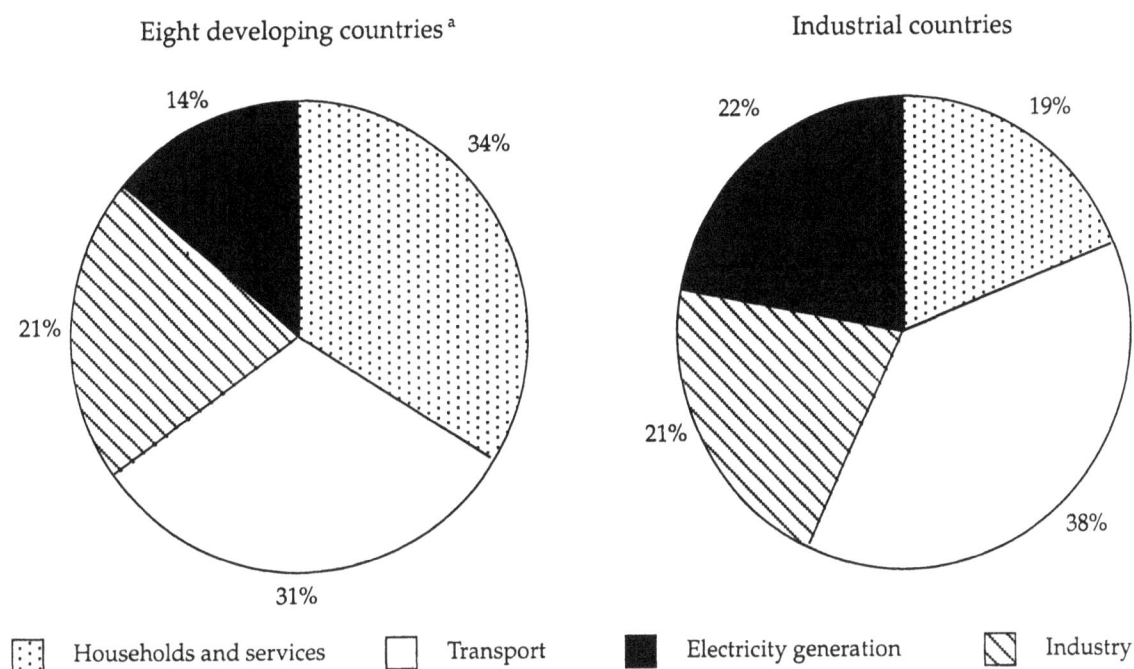

| :: : | Households and services | ☐ Transport | ■ Electricity generation | ◩ Industry |

a. Brazil, China, Indonesia, Malaysia, Pakistan, the Philippines, and Thailand. These countries account for more than 50 percent of the total energy and 35 percent of oil consumed in developing countries.
Source: World Bank (1992, p. 116).

The use of coal and other fossil fuels for electricity generation is increasing rapidly worldwide. Power stations that use fossil fuels constitute two-thirds of the electric power-generating capacity in the world. If this pattern continues without any change in technology, the emission of pollutants will increase 10-fold in the next 40 years.

Industry is using a proportionally larger percentage of commercial energy in developing countries than in the rest of the world. This is because of a growing manufacturing sector and changes in consumption patterns with increasing population and rising living standards.

In developing countries the transport sector is growing rapidly, and so is the pollution from passenger and freight vehicles. About 55 percent of developing countries' total oil consumption is used as fuel for vehicles (World Bank 1992, p. 124). Circumstances in these countries that exacerbate the effects of traffic pollution include concentrated traffic in urban areas, use of lower-quality fuels, and poorly maintained vehicles.

More than 80 percent of the world's total biomass consumption is in developing countries, where it is mostly used for indoor cooking and constitutes nearly 35 percent of total energy use (World Bank 1992, p. 126). The use of biomass for cooking causes severe health problems from indoor air pollution (see chapter 11). It also reduces the availability of dung for fertilizer, and thus contributes to the loss of soil productivity.

Inefficiencies in Energy Use

A significant problem in the energy sector of developing countries is the high degree of inefficiency in production, transmission, distribution, and consumption. For example, in Southeast and South Asian countries, electricity transmission and distribution losses range between 18 to 28 percent, compared with

7 to 8 percent in Japan and the United States during 1981–85 (U.S. Department of Energy 1989). Industrial production processes in developing countries display similar levels of low energy efficiency. Steel manufacturing in inefficient plants, for instance, consumes on average 600 to 1,400 kilograms of oil equivalent per ton of output, compared with an average of 420 to 570 kilograms of oil equivalent per ton of output in the more efficient plants of industrial countries (Ramani 1991). Estimates indicate that about US$30 billion worth of energy is lost annually in transmission and distribution networks in developing countries (World Bank 1992).

Policy Options

Conventional policies in developing countries have often been ineffective in promoting higher levels of energy efficiency. Reasons for this include a combination of government interventions that distort energy markets, for instance, pricing subsidies, tariff barriers, supply monopolies, and so on; of planning processes that tend to focus on the financial, social, and environmental costs without considering the associated investment in environmental impact mitigation, which policymakers see as a tradeoff against investment in economically beneficial activities; and poor consumer awareness of true costs and benefits, for instance, capital costs versus life-cycle costs. The policy response to these issues can be divided into four major components aimed at securing a sustainable energy supply in the long run:

- Increase energy efficiency
- Reduce negative environmental impacts through the use of technology
- Use alternative energy resources
- Implement other complementary policy reforms.

Increasing Energy Efficiency

The most accessible policy response is to increase the efficiency of energy production, transmission, distribution, and consumption. The efficiency concept includes not only the physical (or thermodynamic) efficiency of technical equipment and processes, but also the overall economic efficiency of the energy system. The physical efficiency of technical equipment refers to using lower levels of energy inputs to produce similar or greater output and minimizing losses in existing energy production and use processes. Economic efficiency deals with altering the mix of a given energy system by replacing less efficient fuels with more efficient ones or by introducing more efficient technologies. For example, substituting wood fuels in rural areas with decentralized electric power or replacing low-efficiency incandescent light bulbs with high-efficiency fluorescent lamps.

In many parts of the world, adopting feasible technologies and improving management practices could improve energy efficiency by 10 to 30 percent in two to three decades. If the most advanced technologies available now were to be adopted, some countries could realize energy savings of 50 to 60 percent during the same period (Intergovernmental Panel on Climate Change 1995).

Reducing Negative Environmental Impacts through the Use of Technology

The second component is to make increasing use of technologies that minimize negative environmental effects. If the resource base continues to be fossil fuels, countries can use a range of technologies for specific fuels and can adopt technologies that facilitate switching to another fossil fuel. Improved technologies tend to mitigate local, regional, and global environmental damage.

Local and regional air pollution is largely due to the combustion of fossil fuels, which releases particulate matter and sulfur and nitrogen oxides. The available options for addressing this problem while still using fossil fuels include the following:

- Switching to low-sulfur coals, oil, and gas
- Cleaning coal before combustion
- Controlling emissions
- Improving the efficiency of fuel combustion.

Air pollution, especially nitrogen and carbon dioxide emissions from fossil fuels, includes greenhouse gases that threaten to disrupt the earth's climate by elevating the average temperature. To mitigate this, the conversion of fossil fuels should be more efficient to reduce carbon dioxide emissions. Fossil fuels are characterized by varying ratios of carbon to hydrogen. Switching to fuels with a lower carbon content would result in lower carbon dioxide emissions. Of all fossil fuels, natural gas has the lowest carbon dioxide emissions per unit of energy; however, switching to gas requires enormous infrastructure investments, and a major determining factor will be whether gas is available in the country or is readily available from neighboring countries. An alternative approach involves switching to nonfossil sources of energy.

Using Alternative Energy Sources

The use of most renewable energy sources would virtually eliminate emissions of greenhouse gases. The major alternative resources that are available include hydroelectric power; biomass; and wind, solar, geothermal, and ocean energy.

Hydroelectric power still has a large development potential, but poses a series of social and environmental issues that need to be seriously considered, such as resettlement and destruction of natural habitats.

Biomass supplies include municipal solid waste, industrial and agricultural residues, and existing forests and fuelwood plantations. Currently the technology for biomass conversion (municipal solid waste and industrial and agricultural residues) is not well developed, and for it to become competitive will take time. Forest and fuelwood plantations need to be on a large scale and can come into serious conflict with biodiversity preservation.

Solar energy has large potential for the future. Despite its present low level of use, in regions with high solar intensities estimates indicate that this form of energy will become competitive with nuclear power within a decade, and even with fossil fuels in the longer term. When research and development and economies of scale push prices down, it could provide a considerable portion of such countries' electricity and energy needs. Wind power will probably be competitive in some regions in a decade or two.

When local geology permits, geothermal energy can be used for electricity production. Even though this technology is associated with some greenhouse gas emissions, with improved technology these can be virtually eliminated. Ocean energy in the form of tides, waves, and thermal and salinity gradients can be exploited in theory, but harnessing this as a viable source of energy is unlikely in the near future.

Implementing Complementary Policy Reforms

Energy policies tend to have significant negative effects on energy use, thus reforming these policies could be beneficial. First, energy is sold at prices far below its market costs. In developing countries, average energy prices are a third of the supply cost. Underpricing electricity has major implications for both the environment and the economic efficiency of the energy sector, including increased energy demand, insufficient funding for investments, and reduced incentives to change to newer and less-polluting technologies. Second, energy prices are often determined on an average cost price basis. Therefore, the incremental price of energy for increasing consumption (marginal cost) is high after a certain point, yet the average cost does not usually reflect this increase. Third, the environmental costs, for example, the costs of greenhouse gas emissions, of different energy resources and technologies need to be internalized. In the long run, benefits and costs should include variables that are measured in a conventional financial sense, along with others such as social and environmental variables.

Policy decisions on energy systems will often involve making tradeoffs between costs and benefits for different groups at the local, regional, or higher levels. Policies are usually directed toward reducing local and regional air pollution rather than preventing climate change. Many polices aimed at reducing air pollution from energy consumption will also reduce global air pollution, but there are exceptions. For example, when flue gas scrubbers are installed in coal-fired power plants to reduce sulfur emissions, the conversion efficiency is reduced, which results in net carbon emissions (Intergovernmental Panel on Climate Change, Working Group 2 1996). Correcting many of these policy distortions would greatly improve the environmental situation through increased energy efficiency, reduced emissions, and decreased consumption.

Conclusion

The use of fossil fuels as the primary energy source worldwide significantly affects the environment in the form of local and regional air pollution. Such pollution in turn affects human health and ecosystems. Increasing evidence indicates that the use of fossil fuels contributes to global warming. Global energy consumption is concentrated in high-income countries, although consumption levels are on the rise in developing countries. The total consumption of fossil fuels in developing countries is soon expected to exceed that in high-income countries.

Given the rising levels of fossil fuel consumption, new management regimes and alternative energy sources must be integrated to mitigate the negative environmental and health effects associated with the use of fossil fuels. This situation requires action by changing energy efficiency, reducing negative environmental impacts, and implementing policy reforms. Many technologies exist, but to realize efficiency gains they need to be fully integrated into large energy-generating systems. Innovations in using low-cost renewable energy resources are expected, for instance, solar and wind energy.

In addition to technological solutions, policymakers need to focus on correcting energy pricing to internalize environmental damage. The vital issue for policymakers, planners, and individuals is to use energy efficiency (financial, economic, and environmental) as a major criterion for choosing resources, products, services, and technology.

References

Intergovernmental Panel on Climate Change. 1995. *Climate Change 1995: Impacts, Adaptations, and Mitigation of Climate Changes: Scientific-Technical Analyses.* Cambridge, U.K.: Cambridge University Press.

Intergovernmental Panel on Climate Change, Working Group 2. 1996. *Technologies, Policies, and Measures for Mitigating Climate Change.* Technical Paper no. 1. Geneva: Intergovernmental Panel on Climate Change Secretariat.

Ramani, K. V. 1991. "A Review of Policies for Energy Efficiency in Asian Developing Countries." In Peter Hills, ed., *Energy Efficiency: Hong Kong's Challenge for the '90s.* Hong Kong, China: Hong Kong Institution of Engineers.

U.S. Department of Energy. 1989. *Energy Technology for Developing Countries: Issues for the U.S. National Energy Strategy.* Washington, D.C.

World Bank. 1990. *World Development Report 1990.* New York: Oxford University Press.

_____. 1992. *World Development Report 1992.* New York: Oxford University Press.

_____. 1997. *World Development Indicators.* Washington, D.C.

Other Recommended Readings

Asian Pacific Development Center. 1990. *Decade of Discovery: Responding to Development Needs in the Asian-Pacific.* Kuala Lumpur, Malaysia.

Chantavorapap, S. 1990. "Review of National Energy Policy and R&D Experience in Thailand." In K. V. Ramani, ed., *Energy Research and Development Strategies for Asian Developing Countries*. Kuala Lumpur, Malaysia: Asian and Pacific Development Center.

Goldemberg, Jose, and others. 1987. *Energy for a Sustainable World*. New Delhi: Wiley-Eastern.

Hills, Peter, and K. V. Ramani. 1990. *Energy Systems and the Environment: Approaches to Impact Assessment in Asian Developing Countries*. Kuala Lumpur, Malaysia: Asian and Pacific Development Center.

Katzman, Martin K. and others. 1990. *The Prospects for Energy Efficiency Improvements in Developing Countries*. Oak Ridge, California: Oak Ridge National Laboratory and Lawrence Berkeley Laboratory.

Munasinghe, M. 1990. *Electric Power Economics*. London: Butterworth.

Peek, P. 1988. "How Equitable Are Rural Developmental Projects?" *International Labor Review* 127(1): 73–89.

Rhee, S. Y. 1990. "Energy Policy Experiences in Asian Developing Countries." In K. V. Ramani, ed., *Energy Research and Development Strategies for Asian Developing Countries*. Kuala Lumpur, Malaysia: Asian and Pacific Development Center.

United Nations. 1991. *World Population Projects*. New York.

United Nations Development Programme. 1991. *Human Development Report*. London: Oxford University Press.

Wilbanks, Thomas J. 1990. *Institutional Issues in Energy R&D Strategies for Developing Countries*. Oak Ridge, California: Oak Ridge National Laboratory.

World Bank. 1990. *Capital Expenditures for Electric Power in the Developing Countries in the 1990s*. Energy Series Paper no. 2. Washington, D.C.

World Resources Institute. 1996. *World Resources: A Guide to the Global Environment*. New York: Oxford University Press.

9

Trade and the Environment

Trade among countries can have a significant influence on the environment and on the sustainability of their natural resource bases. The net effect of international trade on the environment is unclear. Changes in economic output and composition due to trade have varying effects on both the source and sink functions of the natural resource base. Expanding trade to external markets implies a number of changes to an economy. Some of the general effects of trade-induced growth are caused by increased economic activity and inflows of foreign capital (scale effect), changes in the composition of economic output (composition effect), and access to expertise and international production standards (technique effect). Others are more specific in nature and depend on the area of export specialization.

Links among Trade, Economics, and the Environment

Complex links exist between trade and the environment. Trade tends to have general effects on both the structure and growth of a national economy. First, in many low- and middle-income countries, it can serve as one of the primary engines of economic growth. Second, trade helps to optimize the efficiency of resource use, which is critical for sustainability. Countries tend to specialize in exporting goods that are relatively abundant (assuming little intervention by the government and the existence of free markets). Third, increased growth can lead to higher standards of living, which may increase the demand for environmental services, for example, clean water and air, well-preserved protected areas).

However, trade neglects the environment the same way domestic markets fail to take environmental losses into account. This is because the use (or abuse) of environmental and natural resources is not properly priced in the market. The reason for this is that the environment tends to be a nonrival, nonexclusive good that eludes market prices. The term nonrival implies that the consumption of a good or service by one individual does not reduce the amount that remains for other consumers, and a nonexclusive good is one to which property rights have not been assigned, hence no one is excluded from consuming it (Randall 1987). Casual observations may suggest that environmental problems intensify with increased trade; however, these problems are not linked to trade as such. Rather, they are due to trade-induced growth and development in general. Government policies that reduce market distortions, support strong property rights, promote laws and regulations that govern the use of natural resources and the environment, and support the formation of a well-educated labor force are the most powerful way to promote sustainable development.

The economywide effects of trade and the environment are mixed. Insofar as trade makes economies wealthier, it can be considered beneficial to the environment, because wealthier societies are more willing to pay to protect the environment (Lucas, Wheeler, and Hettige 1992; Radetzki 1992). However, as economic activity increases, countries must take some precautions, as more materials and energy will be consumed, which can result in environmental degradation and pollution. Even if wealthier societies prefer improved environmental quality, irreversible environmental damage can occur (Holling and others 1994).

Economywide Effects

Figure 9.1 illustrates the relationship between trade and the environment. On a macroeconomic level, one major effect of trade is its tendency to increase economic activity, which leads to three broad effects:

Based on presentations by Mohan Munasinghe and Tamara Belt.

Figure 9.1.   *Trade and the Environment*

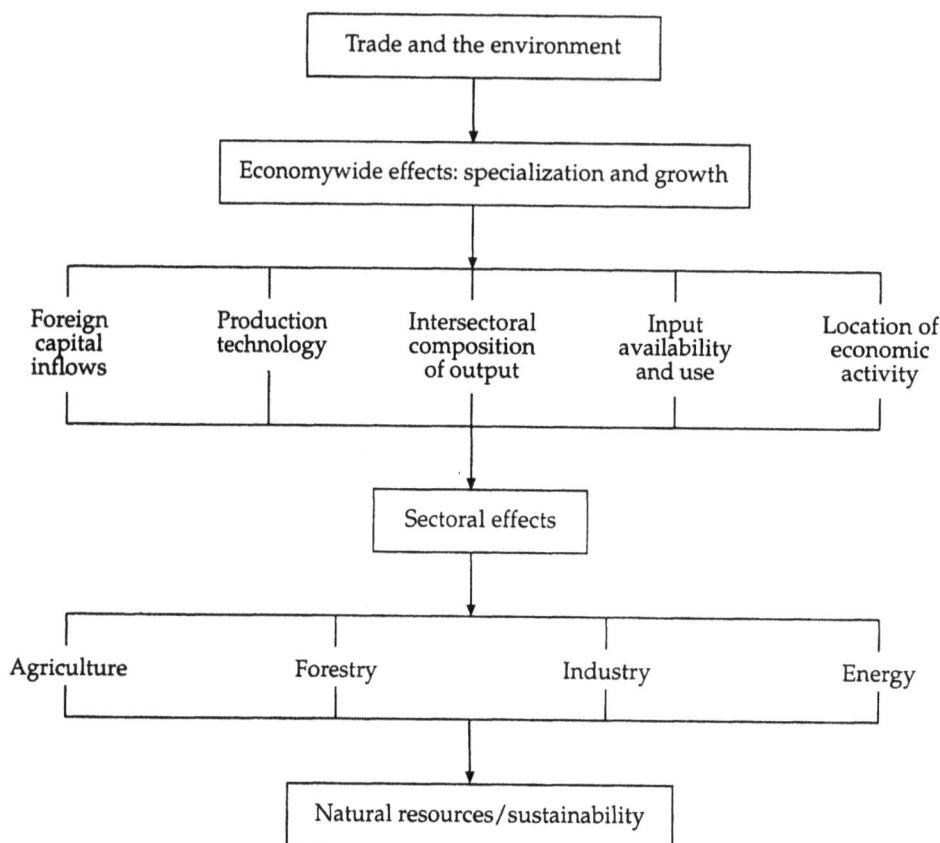

Source: Authors.

those of scale, composition, and technique. Increased economic activity motivates economywide changes that can have environmental impacts, such as

- Increased foreign capital inflows (scale)
- Changes in production processes and use of technology (technique)
- Changes in the intersectoral composition of output (composition)
- Changes in input availability and use (scale and composition)
- Changes in the location of economic activity (scale and composition).

FOREIGN CAPITAL INFLOWS. Increased trade results in greater inflow of capital into the economy. This can contribute positively to sustainable development, because it permits the purchase of manufactured capital goods and improved technology. The result is increased productivity. Expansions in trade often occur after currency devaluation, which may lead to excessive extraction of natural resources, for instance, deforestation for increased agricultural production, cattle ranching, or timber processing.

PRODUCTION TECHNOLOGY. The environment can be positively affected by trade, as it tends to increase access to, and sometimes the diffusion of, more advanced, environmentally friendly technologies. These technologies may use materials more efficiently, either by producing more output with the same level of input, by producing less waste, or by reusing waste. Technological changes can also result in future productivity gains and less pressure on the environment. Some evidence suggests that Latin American economies that are relatively open to trade are more likely to adopt cleaner production technologies than closed economies (Birdsall and Wheeler 1991; Hettige, Muthukumara, and Wheeler 1997).

However, one cannot assume that the relationship between trade and the environment is positive: more sophisticated industrial processes could well lead to increased toxic and hazardous pollutants. The evidence on this is inconclusive, however. In some cases scale effects may outweigh abatement effects (see Hettige, Muthukumara, and Wheeler 1997). As the scale and rate of growth increases, environmental degradation may outpace environmental gains made by cleaner technologies. Although processes may become less polluting, the absolute amount of pollutants may strain the carrying capacity of ecosystems. For example, the United States, which represents about 5 percent of the world's population, is responsible for 20 to 30 percent of the world's emissions of major ozone-degrading compounds.

INTERSECTORAL COMPOSITION OF OUTPUT. Depending on the nature of the export activity, trade will have varied effects on the intersectoral composition of output. Economic activity may shift to sectors in which a country has a relative advantage and may lead to the expansion of the most efficient industries, that is, to better use of capital, natural resource, and human endowments. Increased specialization brought about by trade may have implications for developing countries, because their stock of natural capital tends to be relatively large. This may induce a shift to production processes that use comparatively more natural capital, which may be beneficial. For example, the initial analysis of the North American Free Trade Agreement shows that increased trade in Mexico resulted in increased specialization in labor-intensive and agricultural activities that required fewer energy inputs and generated less hazardous waste per unit of output.

Some of the more rapidly growing low- and middle-income countries are facing structural changes that are affecting the environment in different ways. With increasing investments in the industrial sector and the growth of the transport sector, concern about the so-called brown areas of environmental problems, such as pollution and toxic and hazardous wastes, is increasing. The North American Free Trade Agreement offers another example. Truck traffic across the U.S.-Mexico border is expected to expand from 1.8 million commercial vehicle crossings in 1990 to 8 million in 2000. The negative environmental impacts are colossal, with concomitant increases in air pollution, noise, and congestion (Interagency Task Force 1992).

INPUT AVAILABILITY AND USE. Another general effect of trade on the environment is the availability and use of raw materials as inputs into the production of traded goods. These effects can be beneficial or damaging depending on the extraction methods, the transportation of inputs, and the production processes, all of which can be positively influenced by strong property rights, laws and regulations that govern the use of natural resources and the environment, and government policy that reduces market distortions.

THE LOCATION OF ECONOMIC ACTIVITY. Trade can also affect the environment in terms of the location of the economic activity, which determines whether rapid urbanization, increased pressures on arable agricultural lands and forests, or intensive fishing in inland lakes or off the coasts will occur. Once again, the effects that these shifts may have on the environment can be mitigated by assigning strong property rights and by implementing sensible government policies.

Sectoral Changes

Early arguments against trade were leveled at natural resource degradation caused by intensive agriculture, forestry, and mining activities. Traditionally, developing countries exported primary commodities, such as agricultural products, fish, and timber, which translated into enormous environmental losses not only in terms of natural resource depletion, but also in terms of the goods and services the resource provided, for instance, carbon sequestration, watershed maintenance, and use of organic waste to fertilize soils. Today, exports from developing countries increasingly consist of a higher proportion of processed and manufactured goods and a lower proportion of primary products (World Bank 1997, p. 198). Therefore, the effects of trade are becoming more complex, and range from potential losses of natural resources such as land, water, and biodiversity to environmental degradation, such as water and air pollution and land degradation.

Thus the effects of trade on the environment are mixed, and much depends on the composition of exports, on government policy, and on the ability of markets and government intervention to price natural resources properly. These effects are of a specific nature and must be discussed at the national, subnational, and local levels. One possibility is that trade could increase exiting distortions, particularly when environmental resources are underpriced.

General Agreement on Tariffs and Trade, World Trade Organization, and Environmental Management

As mentioned earlier, the economywide effects of trade on the environment are varied, and much depends on production expansion, government policy, and property rights. This section will move to the international level to discuss how the General Agreement on Tariffs and Trade (GATT), and now the World Trade Organization (WTO), have treated the environment in trade disputes. Besides these organizations, the strongest potential areas for trade to lead to improved environmental management is in creating markets for pollution of the global commons and promoting the preservation of critical and unique biodiversity. Currently, these kind of efforts are realized through international environmental conventions or innovative bilateral agreements (see chapter 10).

In 1995 the WTO was created to succeed the GATT. The WTO is an administrative body where multilateral trade agreements are negotiated and international trade disputes are settled. The WTO Committee on Trade and the Environment has made environmental components central to the work of the WTO.

The degree to which the WTO allows for environmental considerations depends largely on how its regulations are interpreted. An examination of trade disputes concerning environmental issues suggests that the WTO does not favor the use of trade restrictions to further environmental objectives. They consider the overall reduction of protectionist trade barriers to be a priority, and conservation as secondary.

Trade Restrictions: The Case of Unidirectional Externality

Countries often use trade restrictions to redress externalities that occur when imports fail to meet domestic environmental standards (unidirectional externality). This type of externality in trade is said to occur if it arises when the good is consumed in the importing country. For example, in 1989 the United States temporarily banned the importation of fruit from Chile after a health scare caused by a shipment of Chilean grapes that was contaminated with a pesticide. Thus under current WTO conditions and agreements, trade restrictions are acceptable when externalities arise from the consumption of a product.

Conversely, trade restrictions are not allowed if they are redressing an externality that arises during the production process in the exporting country, for example, the hardwood trade and its connection with deforestation. This is the case even if the exporting country does not recognize an externality to itself, but the importing country deems the resulting environmental degradation to be unacceptable.

Environmentalists argue that looking at the situation solely from the point of view of the products' characteristics ignores the full environmental costs associated with the process and product and prevents the internalization of those costs.

The Case of Mutual Externality

Mutual externalities arise when the pollution from an exporting nation affects a common resource, such as the atmosphere, the oceans, or the ozone layer. Typically, controlling such externalities requires an international agreement, and such agreements may use trade sanctions to ensure mutual compliance and to prevent free riders. For the WTO, the issue becomes how to determine the need for such measures. Proponents argue that the need for trade restriction arises because an agreement imposes costs on the participating parties that nonparticipating parties avoid. Thus participants may suffer a comparative disadvantage. In such circumstances, only collectively enforced trade restrictions will produce the desired results. For example, the Montreal Protocol on the protection of the ozone layer contains a provision to ban the trade of products that use chlorofluorocarbons during the production process. While this does not appear to be in keeping with the WTO's view that only the product, and not the production process, is relevant, a clause permits distinguishing collective discrimination against nonsignatories from other restrictions in international agreements. This suggests that trade restrictions under international agreements would generally be compatible with the WTO.

A well-known example where the GATT did not support international environmental concerns is the case of tuna imports from Mexico to the United States. In 1991 the United States amended its Marine Mammal Act to restrict imports of tuna that were caught using purse-seine fishing methods. The argument was that trawlers using purse-seine fishing methods caught more dolphins than U.S. fishing trawlers, which used other fishing methods. The restriction was confined to the eastern Pacific where, the United States claimed, the dolphin was endangered. This restriction had a major impact on Mexican fishermen, but did not affect U.S. fishermen, who had largely given up fishing in that area. Mexico appealed to the GATT on several grounds, including that the measure was designed primarily to protect U.S. fishermen, and that Mexican nets killed much fewer dolphins than had been killed in the past by the U.S. fishing fleet. The issues in the case were as follows:

- Was the restriction imposed primarily to conserve dolphins or to protect the industry?
- Was the restriction necessary for conservation?
- Did the relevant articles in the GATT cover processes (in this case, fishing methods) as opposed to products?

The GATT ruled that trade restrictions could not be justified if they related to the process of production rather than to the product itself. Also, it said that an externality—in this case the U.S. concern for protecting wildlife—cannot be considered for restrictions if it does not occur within the territory of the country concerned. Thus the GATT overruled the U.S. trade sanctions.

The WTO's distinction between environmental damage arising from the consumption of a product and from its production process does not seem relevant from an economics standpoint because, after all, both represent a form of an externality. In relation to the WTO's lack of provision for the latter, discussions have taken place outside the WTO about the need for more harmonized regulations for production processes. One major argument for harmonizing environmental standards for production processes across nations is that variable standards discourage competitiveness in the nation with the strictest standards and encourage polluting industries to migrate to countries with the lowest environmental standards. The issue is linked to the more general one of whether environmental regulations cause firms to lose their competitive advantage (see box 9.1).

There appears to be a case for establishing an international code relating to product standards that could act as nontariff barriers. However, harmonizing environmental standards worldwide may not necessarily improve the environment. This is due to different geographies, industrial concentrations, and environmental attributes. In any case, simply formulating standards does not mean that countries will comply with them. Therefore, when standards are used, the aim should be to foster sustainability with growth within a specific country. These standards should be relevant to local conditions and should apply to both local and international firms.

Policy Implications of Trade and the Environment

One of the benefits of trade is that it increases economic activity and can have a positive effect on growth. Trade may also shift production to areas of relative efficiency, thereby leading to a better use of endowments within a country. Trade may also lead to higher living standards and increase the demand for environmental services. Increased economic activity can also result in more funding and stronger institutions

Box 9.1. Environmental Regulations and Competitiveness

Little empirical evidence supports the argument that competitiveness and trade would suffer from environmental policy. In the manufacturing sector, where environmental regulations are more prevalent than in the agriculture sector, empirical and case study evidence show that environmental regulations have had no significant effects on trade patterns and competitiveness. Some studies have found that regulatory abatement costs amount to only a small proportion of total costs. The average for U.S. exports has been estimated at 1.75 percent of total costs, compared to 1.50 percent for imports into the United States. Therefore, industry relocation to countries with loose pollution regulations is not justified. However, investigators have found that industries relocate because of a variety of other reasons, not just pollution regulations, namely:

- Market factors
- Worker safety regulations
- Mandatory relocation, as in the case of manufacturers of hazardous chemicals.

Other adaptations are generally more cost-effective than relocation, for instance:

- Introducing technological innovations
- Using new raw materials or substitute products
- Reclaiming raw materials
- Implementing tighter processing and quality controls.

Moreover, international comparisons of environmental regulations show that countries have tended to introduce regulations at roughly the same time and at the same levels of stringency; therefore, they tend not to be discriminatory.

One area that could affect trade and competitiveness is the burgeoning concept of ecolabeling. The purpose of ecolabeling is to promote the consumption and production of environmentally more friendly products by providing consumers with information about environmental impacts incurred during the production process. Although such programs are voluntary, they may affect international competitiveness by isolating those countries or companies who are unaware of these initiatives, and may serve as an obstacle to trade. Also the emergence of a large number of national ecolabeling schemes in industrial countries could affect developing country producers, particularly small-scale exporters, who will have problems adjusting to the requirements of ecolabels of different markets.

for environmental protection. However, this does not happen automatically, and trade does not necessarily lead to improved environmental quality. Therefore, sound economic policies, secure property rights, and strong environmental institutions are needed to correct market and policy failures so that countries can avoid environmental externalities as much as possible.

Rapid economic growth can also have negative effects on the environment. Increased economic activity can result in the rapid consumption of natural resources and increased environmental pollution. However, policy can help mitigate these effects by strengthening property rights, implementing sound economic policy, introducing targeted policies that protect the most fragile ecosystems and areas of rapid degradation, and increasing environmental education and awareness. On the international level, increased globalization can significantly benefit the environment if mechanisms are put in place to address externalities in both production processes and product markets.

The policy implication for developing countries is that the intensification of natural resource-based activities may lead to irreversible damage. This will call for policies that focus on the primary sector. Preemptive policy could take the form of strengthening property rights; educating people about sustainable production methods; and imposing environmental taxes on activities that will affect regional ecosystems, for instance, deforestation, which affects hydrological cycles and nutrient recycling. When increased economic activity occurs in the industrial sector, policy will need to focus, among other things, on a mix of market-based instruments, local participation, and private-public sector partnerships.

Another area of focus should be to optimize the benefits of trade. For instance, tax credits could be used to encourage the transfer of new technology and adoption of more efficient production methods.

Public-private partnerships can also be stimulated through the formation of joint research and development centers that focus on cleaner technologies and waste recycling.

The implications of the numerous environmental conventions (see chapter 10) and of the formation of the WTO on correcting externalities are enormous. Both have embraced the notion of pursuing policies that benefit economic and environmental globalization. Environmental globalization, in the sense of raising environmental concerns to a global level and engaging in efforts either bilaterally or multilaterally to protect the global commons, is clearly advantageous.

Conclusion

Trade and increased economic activity can be beneficial or detrimental to the environment. The complex links between increased economic activity and inflows of foreign capital and expertise make ascertaining the net benefits of trade for the environment impossible. It seems, however, that increased prosperity tends to increase interest in protecting the environment, yield more funds to pay for environmental damage, result in the use of cleaner technologies and more efficient production practices, and encourage the formation of stronger institutions focused on environmental protection.

The decisions of the WTO with respect to the environment have been ambiguous. The GATT and WTO were formed mainly to promote trade, and environmental concerns only surfaced recently. Thus the WTO continues to be primarily concerned with promoting free trade, with environmental protection in second place. Nevertheless, the WTO has supported some issues linked to international agreements, such as the ban on trade of products made with using chlorofluorocarbons. Also, a recently established environmental focus by the WTO may result in greener policy shifts.

The impact of free trade policies on the environment are often unclear because of the complex links between trade, growth, and the environment. Given the potentially high gains from free trade, policies that restrict trade for environmental purposes must be approached with caution. Moreover, environmental regulations will not necessarily lead to reduced competitiveness. Empirical evidence from the manufacturing sector has shown that costs for environmental compliance are only a small portion of total production costs. Policies should focus on sustainably managing trade-induced growth through implementing sound macroeconomic and sectoral policies, strengthening property rights, fostering local participation and private-public sector partnerships, and increasing environmental education and awareness. Obviously, countries must rank their priorities among these depending on their particular economic situation and the composition of export growth. No blueprint for action is available given the present structure of the global marketplace, and environmental management must first start at the local and national levels.

References

Birdsall, Nancy, and David Wheeler. 1991. "Openness Reduces Industrial Pollution in Latin America: The Missing Pollution Haven Effect." Paper prepared for the World Bank Symposium on International Trade and the Environment, November 21–22, Washington, D.C.

Hettige, Hemamala, Muthukumara Mani, and David Wheeler. 1997. "Industrial Pollution in Economic Development (Kuznets Revisited)." Policy Research Working Paper no. 1876. World Bank, Washington, D.C.

Holling, C. S., D. W. Schindler, B. W. Walker, and J. Roughgarden. 1994. "Biodiversity in the Functioning of Ecosystems: An Ecological Primer and Synthesis." In V. Perrings, K. G. Maler, C. Folke, C. S. Holling, and B. O. Jansson, eds., *Biodiversity Loss: Ecological and Economic Issues*. Cambridge, U.K.: Cambridge University Press.

Interagency Task Force. 1992. "Review of U.S.-Mexico Environmental Issues." Coordinated by the Office of the U.S. Trade Representative. Washington, D.C.

Lucas, R. E. B., David Wheeler, and Hemamala Hettige. 1992. "Economic Growth and the Environment." In Patrick Low, ed., *International Trade and the Environment*. Discussion Paper no. 159. Washington, D.C.: World Bank.

Radetzki, Marian. 1992. "Economic Growth and the Environment." In Patrick Low, ed., *International Trade and the Environment*. Discussion Paper no. 159. Washington, D.C.: World Bank.

Randall, Alan. 1987. *Resource Economics: An Economic Approach to Natural Resource and Environmental Policy*. New York: John Wiley & Son.

World Bank. 1997. *World Development Indicators*. Washington, D.C.

Other Recommended Readings

Barbier, E., and others. 1994. *The Economics of the Tropical Timber Trade*. London: Earthscan.

Dean, Judith M. 1992. "Trade and the Environment. A Survey of the Literature." Background paper for the *World Development Report 1992*. World Bank, Washington, D.C.

Grainger, A. 1992. *Controlling Tropical Deforestation*. London: Earthscan.

Grossman, Gene M., and Alan B. Krueger. 1991. "Environmental Impacts of a North American Free Trade Agreement." Working Paper Series no. 3914. National Bureau of Economic Research, Cambridge, Massachusetts.

Johnstone, Nick. 1995. "Trade Liberalization, Economic Specialization, and the Environment." *Ecological Economics* 14(3): 165–73.

Low, Patrick. 1992. *International Trade and the Environment*. Discussion Paper no. 159. World Bank: Washington, D.C.

Munasinghe, Mohan, ed. 1996. *Environmental Impacts of Macroeconomic and Sectoral Policies*. Washington, D.C.: World Bank.

Munasinghe, Mohan, and Wilfrido Cruz. 1994. *Economywide Polices and the Environment*. Washington, D.C.: World Bank.

Pearce, David W., and Jeremy J. Warford. 1993. *World Without End*. New York: Oxford University Press.

Shiva, Vandana, and Vanaja Ramprasad. 1993. *Cultivating Diversity*. Dehra Dun, India: Natraj Publishers.

Swift, M. J., and J. M. Anderson. 1992. "Biodiversity and Ecosystem Function in Agricultural Systems." In E. D. Schultz, and H. A. Mooney, eds., *Biodiversity and Ecosystem Function*. Berlin: Springer-Berlag.

United States Congress, Office of Technology Assessment. 1992. *Trade and Environment: Conflicts and Opportunities*. Document no. OTA-BP-ITE-94. Washington, D.C.: U.S. Government Printing Office.

World Bank. 1992. *World Development Report 1992*. New York: Oxford University Press.

World Commission on Environment and Development. 1987. *Our Common Future*. New York: Oxford University Press.

World Resources Institute. 1994. *World Resources 1994–95*. New York: Oxford University Press.

10

Global Environmental Issues

Global environmental issues are becoming a serious area of concern and debate. Unfortunately, concerted action, both at the global and regional levels, has been lacking because of the complexity of environmental problems and because of the inability of political and economic systems to address them. A fundamental reason why countries are reluctant to address these issues is because the abatement or preservation costs to a single country far exceed the benefits. Moreover, like local environmental problems, global environmental problems have spatial and temporal dimensions that transcend administrative and national jurisdictions. In addition, scientific information about global environmental problems is imperfect, and information about the negative effects of the degradation of the global commons and about mitigation efforts is also sparse. Finally, developing countries see the industrial countries as the source of many environmental problems and are therefore reluctant to address some of the issues. Collaboration by countries to address global and transboundary environmental issues is the only way that natural resources, the environment, and biodiversity can be sustainably managed.[1]

A useful method of classifying international environmental problems is in terms of their externalities. An externality exists when one economic agent, in this case a country, imposes a cost or benefit on another agent without providing appropriate compensation. Emissions from fossil fuel consumption (coal, petroleum) are an example of a problem of local origin with a far-reaching impact (and externalities). Impacts from fossil fuel emissions include the following:

- *Local*: contamination of air or soils immediately surrounding the source of emissions
- *Regional*: emissions transported over long distances that descend as acid precipitation, which effects regional ecosystems
- *Global*: emissions contributing to the cumulative buildup of greenhouse gases in the earth's atmosphere.

A different way to classify global issues is according to the range of either their source or impact. For example:

Regional issues	*Global issues*
• Air pollution, acid precipitation	• Greenhouse gases
• Water pollution	• Ozone-depleting substances
• Migrating fish stocks	• Biodiversity
	• Toxic and hazardous wastes
	• Antarctica

The reason why countries will not act alone to deal with fossil fuel emissions is because they are affected disproportionately, and at the same time, some countries pollute more than others.

Table 10.1 presents the different types of unidirectional and reciprocal externalities. Unidirectional externalities occur when one agent imposes damage on another, for example, acid rain may occur because of pollution from one country, yet damage occurs in another. Reciprocal interaction occurs when

---

Based on presentations by R. Clement Jones, G. Hughes, and K. Muir-Lerresche.

1. The term transboundary will be used interchangeably with global or regional, because the objective is to demonstrate how environmental issues transcend political boundaries and why international cooperation is needed on issues such as transboundary externalities (acid rain, climate change) to help solve environmental problems.

different countries impose damage on each other. For example, overgrazing in two contiguous countries can exacerbate the ecosystem integrity of both. In reality, an international externality can be a mix of unidirectional and reciprocal interactions. For example, acid rain may emanate from country A and cause damage to countries B and C. Country A may cause environmental degradation within its own borders, while at the same time suffer damage from countries B and C. Table 10.1 provides more examples of this approach to classification.

Developing Markets for Global Issues

Many actions that a country could take to improve its own environment could also benefit the environments of other nations or of the global community. A purely national comparison of costs and benefits may, however, indicate that the costs do not justify the benefits of an environmental clean-up, because the costs are born nationally, whereas the benefits accrue to the world. Therefore, a need exists to develop markets to try to make polluters pay for environmental and natural resource damage or to compensate those who protect the environment. This requires legal, administrative, and economic frameworks.

In designing policies dealing with the global environment, the following are some of the issues to be addressed:

- To what extent should countries seek environmental improvements beyond levels justified by local or national benefits alone?
- How can such additional efforts be financed?
- What is the correct institutional framework at the regional, national, and local levels to execute and enforce such policies?
- What are the necessary legal agreements?
- How can economic incentives be created to mitigate transboundary pollution and foster improved resource use?

In answering all these questions, people's moral values in relation to natural resources and their willingness to conserve will be critical. Common values about resources are necessary for international compliance on specific actions to be effective. For instance, establishing a ceiling on carbon dioxide emissions is extremely difficult to enforce on a global level. Systems that monitor the emissions of each country

Table 10.1.   *Global Environmental Problems Broken Down by Type of Externality*

Type of externality	Generator and sufferer (number of countries)	Examples
Unidirectional	One => One	United States-Canada, acid rain
	One => Few	Upstream country in multicountry watershed (for example, Danube River), forest fires (Indonesia), radiation (Chernobyl)
	Few => One	Transportation of toxic waste
	Few => Few	Baltic, North Sea whaling, Black Sea
	Few => Many	Whaling, deforestation, forest fires
	Many => Few	Sea level rise (for example, small island developing countries)
Reciprocal	One <=> One	None
	Few <=> Few	Mediterranean, acid rain; migratory stock (Pacific salmon)
	Many <=> Many	Climate change, ozone layer, biodiversity loss

Source: Adapted from Pearce and Warford (1993, p. 328).

would be extremely expensive, both technically and institutionally. Moreover, because no formal enforcement mechanisms exist on the international level, a country could simply ignore its commitment without facing any serious sanctions.

Global environmental problems need to be solved by mutual cooperation between states. Such cooperation needs to include both the transfer of funds to countries that need assistance, as well as agreements on common responsibilities through law making processes. The main issue is to devise an efficient system of incentives that will encourage cooperation. The procurement of funds and the commitment to international agreements will, in the end, be strongly influenced by political will and public opinion in each country. These issues are complicated and must be resolved based on the availability of local resources and the efficiency with which they can be used. Box 10.1 provides an example of a transboundary approach to address a critical environmental issue in Central Asia, the destruction of the Aral Sea Basin, and illustrates how some of the questions were answered.

Box 10.1.   The Aral Sea Program

The Aral Sea basin covers the six states of Afghanistan, Kazakhstan, the Kyrgyz Republic, Tajikistan, Turkmenistan, and Uzbekistan. In 1960 it was the fourth largest inland lake in the world. Since then it has shrunk to less than half its original size because of heavy water withdrawals. This, combined with excessive fertilizer use, lack of adequate drainage, and water pollution from urban and industrial wastes has resulted in tremendous ecological stress. The region is also suffering from economic depression and serious health affects brought about by contaminated drinking water and food.

This crisis motivated the leaders of the five former Soviet Union states to initiate discussions on transboundary cooperation. Through an interstate council and commission, the countries sought assistance from such multilateral agencies as the World Bank and the United Nations Environment Programme to support them in four major areas: (a) stabilizing the environment of the Aral Sea basin, (b) rehabilitating the disaster zone around the sea, (c) improving the management of the water of the Aral Sea basin, and (d) building the capacity of regional institutions to plan and implement these actions.

Regional institutions established by the heads of state were to implement these objectives. These included the Interstate Council for the Aral Sea, the Executive Committee, and the Interstate Fund for the Aral Sea . The Interstate Council consists of 25 senior representatives from the five states. It mediates the resolution of disputes between the member states and decides whether to go ahead with policies, programs, and institutional proposals recommended by the Executive Committee. The Executive Committee is the key organization for developing programs and policies and has been given similar status to that of a state government, with full powers to plan and implement projects approved by the Interstate Council. The Interstate Fund was established to finance the Aral Sea Program and is intended to channel financing from the five basin countries and from donors. In 1997, the Interstate Council and Interstate Fund were merged into a restructured Interstate Fund. There are also regional coordinating commissions for water, technical, ecological, and socioeconomic development concerns.

Although the program is in its infancy, it has major inherent strengths that are not usually found in programs of this kind, namely:

- It is consistent with all previous agreements between the five states.
- Its objectives, concepts, designs, and institutions are based on decisions made by the Interstate Fund and confirmed by the heads of state.
- The priorities for individual projects are consistent with the priorities and program framework endorsed by the basin states, the donors, and the international agencies.
- The Aral Sea crisis has attracted worldwide attention, and international agencies and donor countries have indicated keen interest in supporting the basin countries' cooperative efforts to address it.
- The basin countries have demonstrated their commitment to cooperate, despite their differences about other matters. Their increasing awareness of the economic, social, and ecological effects of the crisis is further cementing this commitment.

International Transfer of Funds

International transfers of financial resources from richer to poorer regions are necessary for investing in environmental policies and projects that will bring mutual gain to all, both giver and receiver. Transfers can be made in many ways. The main channels are through bilateral, multilateral, or some international conventions. The following are some examples:

- Lump sum payments that can be transferred directly to compensate a country for not extracting natural resources or for improving its environmental management. For instance, in 1996 Costa Rica sold its first batch of certifiable tradable offsets. These represent a specific number of units of carbon dioxide gas emissions expressed in carbon equivalent units reduced or sequestered via tree planting. This joint project by Costa Rica and Norway resulted in a contribution of US$2 million from Norway to Costa Rica in exchange for 200,000 certifiable tradable offsets. This benefited Costa Rica, because it received additional funds to protect its forests and expand reforestation, but at the same time Norway benefited from the receipt of certifiable tradable offsets that it could use to cheaply offset its carbon emissions in the event that it became subject to greenhouse gas emissions quotas.
- Compensatory resources that are transferred to a country that engages in less resource degradation and implements more sustainable methods of resource management. The transfer may take the form of technical assistance and grants aimed at environmental action and projects.
- A reduction of debt obligations. International organizations such as The Nature Conservancy or the World Wildlife Fund may use this approach if developing countries agree to reduce their environmental degradation and manage their natural resources in a sustainable way. These approaches are referred to as debt-for-nature swaps. For instance, in 1987 Conservation International orchestrated the first successful debt-for-nature swap with Bolivia. Conservation International acquired US$650,000 of Bolivian commercial bank debt for the discounted price of US$100,000. In return, the Bolivian government agreed to provide operating funds to increase the Beni Biosphere Reserve by 3.7 million acres and to set aside US$250,000 in local currency to manage the reserve. By doing so, the bank improved its debt portfolio by dropping a risky loan; Conservation International leveraged its investment from US$100,000 to US$250,000 and increased the land value under preservation; and the Bolivian government relieved a small portion of its US$4 billion foreign debt in exchange for a new, local obligation (U.S. Department of Agriculture, Forest Service 1994).

The Global Environment Facility (GEF) was established in 1991. It serves as a financial mechanism that provides grant and concessional funds to recipient countries to generate global environmental benefits that national governments would not otherwise fund. The GEF program and projects are managed through three implementing agencies: the United Nations Development Programme, the United Nations Environment Programme, and the World Bank.

The GEF provides financial assistance in four focal areas:

- Climate change
- Ozone layer depletion
- International water resources
- Biodiversity.

Countries may be eligible for GEF funding in one of two ways: (a) if they are eligible for financial assistance through the financial mechanisms of either the Climate Change Convention or the Convention on Biological Diversity, or (b) if they are eligible to borrow from the World Bank or to receive technical assistance grants from the United Nations Development Programme. Activities relating to land degradation, primarily deforestation and desertification as they relate to the four focal areas, are eligible for funding. The GEF's lending program tripled from fiscal 1995 to 1998 (table 10.2), and as of 1997 had financed projects in more than 114 countries.

Table 10.2. *GEF Operational Outputs by Type, Fiscal 1995–98*
(US$ millions)

Type of operation	Fiscal 1995	Fiscal 1996	Fiscal 1997	Fiscal 1998
Long-term operations	88	253	324	370
Enabling activities	10	6	21	17
Short-term measures	37	58	49	15
Total	135	317	394	402

Source: GEF (1997).

International Agreements and Conventions

Other major international efforts to protect the global environment are devised by developing international law. The following six agreements and conventions are important outcomes of this process:

- Montreal Protocol
- Framework Convention for Climate Change
- Basel Convention
- Convention on Combating Desertification
- Convention on Biological Diversity
- Convention on International Trade in Endangered Species (CITES).

Montreal Protocol

The principal international policy instrument for protecting the stratospheric ozone layer is the Montreal Protocol, which was established in 1987 from the framework of the United Nations Convention for the Protection of the Ozone Layer. The protocol outlines states' responsibilities for protecting human health and the environment against the adverse effects of ozone depletion. This landmark international agreement stipulates that the production and use of compounds that deplete ozone in the stratosphere—chlorofluorocarbons, halons, carbon tetrachloride, and methyl chloroform—are to be phased out by 2000.

Framework Convention on Climate Change

In 1988 the World Meteorological Organization and the United Nations Environment Programme set up the Intergovernmental Panel on Climate Change. The panel's mandate was to assess the state of existing knowledge about the climate system and climate change; to assess the environmental, economic, and social impacts of climate change; and to investigate possible response strategies to mitigate the effects of global warming. The panel's first report was released in 1990.

In 1995 the panel released its "Second Assessment Report" with the participation of some 2,000 scientists from around the world. The report (see United Nations Environment Programme 1997) concluded that

- Humanity's emissions of greenhouse gases are likely to cause rapid climate change.
- Climate models predict that the global temperature will rise by 1.0 to 3.5 degrees Celsius by 2100.
- Climate change will have powerful impacts on the global environment.
- Human society will face new risks and pressures because of changing agroecological conditions, changing fish habitats, and rising sea levels, among others.
- People and ecosystems will need to adapt to the future climate regime.
- Stabilizing atmospheric concentrations of greenhouse gases will require a major effort.

The reports by the Intergovernmental Panel on Climate Change have formed the basis of the global response to the threat of global warming. Largely based on this, the United Nations Framework

Convention on Climate Change was drafted. This convention was adopted at the Rio Conference in 1992, and as of mid-1997, 167 countries had ratified the convention. The convention's objectives are to stabilize greenhouse gas concentrations in the atmosphere at a level that does not induce manmade interference with the climate system.

The convention outlines general principles for policy approaches, and recognizes that action needs to be taken irrespective of full scientific certainty about the causes and effects of climate change, because of the danger of irreversible damage. The convention also recognizes that the industrial countries must take the lead in any action. Therefore, in the nonbinding agreement industrial countries are supposed to reduce their emissions to 1990 levels by 2000 and to provide financial resources for technology transfer to developing countries. All countries are required to submit annual data on greenhouse gas emissions and the amount sequestered by environmental sinks, such as oceans and the forests, where carbon dioxide can be stored in substantial quantities. One option many people are considering is creating a market for carbon (see box 10.2).

Basel Convention

The 1989 Basel Convention on the Control of Transboundary Movements of Hazardous Wastes and Their Disposal was designed to eliminate the risks arising from the transboundary movements of hazardous and other wastes. These risks include those arising from the transportation, handling, disposal, and recycling of waste. Central to this process were movements from industrial to developing countries. The convention requires a prior informed consent that must be followed before any export or import is allowed to or from another party. Each party has the right to ban any import or export of hazardous or other wastes.

The basic purposes of the convention are to ensure that states have the full ability to protect their own environment and to enable them to not permit actions within their territory that could cause damage to another country.

Box 10.2.   *Creation of a Carbon Market*

Increasing evidence exists that human activities have been and are currently contributing to climate change. In 1992 more than 150 countries signed the United Nations Framework Convention on Climate Change in the hope of finding ways to mitigate the effects of anthropogenic sources of climate change. International collaboration in reducing carbon emissions and other greenhouse gases is expected to be an efficient way for industrial countries to meet their emission reduction targets. One form of collaboration is a process whereby one party can implement measures jointly with another party in an effort to reduce these emissions. As the costs of reducing carbon emissions are assumed to be relatively cheaper in developing countries (and their Kyoto targets are lower) than those of industrial countries, the latter are expected to pay the developing countries instead of reducing their own emissions. This could be done on a private sector level or based on agreements between nations.

The existence of supply (carbon offsets in low-cost countries) and demand (obligated high-cost countries) thus creates a market for buying and selling carbon offsets. However, four conditions need to be met for this concept to work: (a) a commitment among countries to binding emissions reductions; (b) the existence of relatively high marginal costs of abatement of carbon in the industrial countries and low marginal costs in other countries; (c) an institutional framework for the obligated countries to purchase carbon offsets from the developing countries, and then to receive credit for these offsets achieved outside their borders toward their own reduction obligations; and (d) the verification of offsets. Two additional important points also need to be considered: first, transaction costs must remain low, which is unlikely because of the complexity of this kind of market; and second, risk will be an essential factor, with the main risk being protecting forests from wars, fires, natural disasters, parasites, and humans.

Source: Global Climate Change Unit (1997).

Convention on Combating Desertification

The objectives of the 1994 International Convention to Combat Desertification in Countries Experiencing Serious Drought and/or Desertification are to combat desertification and mitigate the effects of drought in affected countries. The objectives are to be met through effective action at all levels, supported by international cooperation. As of May 1995, 115 countries had signed the convention, and 29 had ratified it.

Desertification processes are closely linked to the conservation and use of biodiversity and international water resources, to climate change, and to global warming. The wide gap between economic planning and the implementation of actions for combating desertification calls for a well-defined, integrated, international and national approach. Consequently, the convention explicitly recognizes the need to

- Integrate desertification strategies with poverty reduction initiatives to reflect the relationship between poverty and the environment
- Develop an integrated, cross-cultural approach to sustainable management of natural resources
- Prepare, publicize, and implement national action plans
- Promote sound policies and strengthen institutional frameworks
- Establish or strengthen food security systems, including marketing and storage
- Establish appropriate financial mechanisms.

Convention on Biological Diversity

The Convention on Biological Diversity, signed in 1992, represents a dramatic step forward in the conservation of biological diversity, the sustainable use of its components, and the fair and equitable sharing of benefits arising from the use of genetic resources. Furthermore, for the first time the international community has taken a comprehensive rather than a sectoral approach to conservation. The convention recognizes that biodiversity and biological resources should be conserved for reasons of ethics, economic benefit, and human survival.

The convention goes beyond the conservation of biodiversity as such and the sustainable use of biological resources, to encompass such issues as access to genetic resources and biotechnology. In addition, it recognizes the uneven distribution of biodiversity around the globe. If biodiversity is to be conserved, it imposes a heavier burden on the South. To carry such a burden, developing countries need additional contributions from, and increased partnerships with, the industrial countries.

The convention requires parties to integrate biodiversity conservation into national decisionmaking, for example, national biodiversity strategies, and to adopt measures aimed at avoiding or minimizing adverse impacts on biological diversity. It also requires parties to promote the sharing of information, to adopt incentive measures, to undertake research and training, to encourage public education, and to carry out environmental impact assessments on projects likely to have significant adverse effects on biological diversity.

Convention on International Trade in Endangered Species

The conversion of indigenous habitat to farming, mining, and industry is the principal cause of the loss of biological diversity, but monoculture, climate change, trade, and other factors contribute. International trade in wildlife is a multibillion dollar industry. The trade in indigenous plants and animals can encourage habitat retention, and thus contribute to species conservation or, if unsustainable, it can contribute to the decline of endangered species. The objective of CITES is to conserve wildlife and prevent international trade from threatening species with extinction. As of early 1997, 125 counties were members of the convention. Signatory countries have joined together to ban trade through the use of government permits.

Protection is divided into two main categories. The first category includes the most endangered species. No trade permits are issued for this group except in exceptional circumstances. The second category consists of those species at serious risk that might become extinct if trade is not controlled. In most countries custom officers are charged with enforcing the convention, and governments are required to submit reports to the secretariat in Switzerland. Member states hold biannual meetings to discuss changes in the lists of protected species. Representatives of nongovernmental organizations and trade associations participate in the meetings.

CITES has brought a wide measure of control to the wildlife trade. Many wildlife traders, who at first regarded CITES with suspicion, are now cooperating because they have realized that well-controlled trade is in their interests. Some are even providing funds for surveys and projects. However, the treaty remains subject to considerable debate, and some countries feel that they are being penalized for successfully protecting their wildlife. Most compelling is the situation in the Southern African countries. The African elephant, which is endangered in other parts of Africa, is not under threat in Southern Africa. Therefore, these countries consider that they are being unduly punished for two reasons: (a) the losses of potential revenues from sustainable elephant hunting; and (b) the preservation of the elephant to the detriment of ecosystems, which is resulting in the disappearance of other critical biodiversity. In response to this critique, the 10th session of the Conference of the Parties, held in June 1997, decided to temporarily lift the ban on ivory trade for Botswana, Namibia, and Zimbabwe to allow them to sell their stockpiles of ivory in 1999 if they take steps to prevent illegal trafficking in ivory.

Opponents who wish to see CITES rewritten have two fundamental arguments. First, some hunting of wildlife can be compatible with conservation. The classic example is the rhinoceros in South Africa. Ranchers began to breed the white rhinoceros, which faced near extinction in 1950 and now numbers more than 7,000. The second argument states that legal trade in wildlife is sustainable and does not automatically result in endangerment, and that illegal trade has always existed and the lack of political will, on both the supply and demand side, accounts for its growth. Southern Africa, the primary region calling for a lifting of the ivory ban, states that it has the political will and has developed methods to mark tusks that will be the equivalent of hallmarks for gold or serial numbers for bank notes and can prevent illegal trade.

National Policy for Global Issues

Incorporating global considerations into national policies can pose somewhat of a challenge to policymakers. Not only are such considerations a recent addition to the policy agenda, they are mostly viewed as being in conflict with national interests. Therefore garnering support for them both from within the government and from the public in general can be difficult. There is also tension between the North and the South on various issues. However, this situation is changing rapidly. The development of international consensus for global environmental agreements, as well as the increasing general awareness among the general public and the private sector, is turning things around. This general consensus about the importance of the long-term survival of ecosystems, and ultimately of humanity, is a major motivator for including global issues on the national agenda.

Countries with limited financial resources have other more immediate advantages from participating in such global policy work as ratifying global environmental conventions. First, by doing so, they will be eligible to receive funds such as GEF funds, and technology will be transferred to them to allow them to initiate projects designed to help them meet convention targets. This can give countries access to the latest clean technologies, and will also help them solve more immediate local environmental problems and improve the level of technical knowledge and competence within the country. Second, their trade relationships could benefit. Increasingly, the environmental standards of both products and their manufacturing processes will become part of trade restrictions, whether by obligation or because they are demand-driven. Third, with consumer attention focused on the environmental friendliness of products, companies can win a great deal of goodwill by voluntarily developing a green profile for their products and modes of production.

Conclusion

Transboundary environmental problems are complicated to solve because no single authority can issue and enforce appropriate policies and regulations. Furthermore, solutions must accommodate large variations in the balance of benefits and costs to different countries. Because of market failure (externalities), other mechanisms must be established to protect the global environment. Some of these efforts must take place on a regional scale, such as the clean-up of rivers and coastal zones. Others are clearly of a global nature, such as greenhouse gas emissions, which may lead to global warming, biodiversity loss, and damage to complex global ecosystems. These issues require responses at the global level.

Transferring funds to developing countries is one important way to enable them to address environmental problems of a global nature. These countries usually face such significant environmental problems at the local and national levels that mechanisms have been created to transfer funds that they can use to address global issues. One such mechanism is the GEF.

The major goals of the conventions to address environmental threats are to protect the ozone layer of the stratosphere, stabilize the level of greenhouse gases in the atmosphere at levels that do not alter the climate, combat desertification and mitigate the effects of drought, and conserve the biological diversity of the world by protecting habitats and stopping trade in threatened species. The combined goals of these conventions are no small task. It will require substantial efforts by all countries to implement the necessary measures. Governments will need a great deal of support from their people to take the first bold steps of considering time spans of decades and centuries in their policies in addition to their electoral periods.

References

GEF (Global Environment Facility). 1997. *GEF Corporate Budget for FY98*. Document no. GEF/C.9/4. Washington, D.C.

Global Climate Change Unit. 1997. *Guidelines for Climate Change Global Overlays*. Environment Department Papers no. 047. Washington, D.C.: World Bank, Global Environment Division.

Pearce, David W., and Jeremy J. Warford. 1993. *World Without End*. New York: Oxford University Press.

United Nations Environment Programme. 1997. Web site updated March 1997: http://www.unep.ch/iucc/rio.html.

U.S. Department of Agriculture, Forest Service. 1994. International Forestry Issue Brief no 9. September. Web site: http://www.fs.fed.us/global/international/policy/issuebriefs/issue9.html.

Other Recommended Readings

Barbier, E. B., J. C. Burgess, T. M. Swanson, and D. W. Pearce. 1990. *Elephants, Economics, and Ivory*. London: Earthscan Publications.

Child, Graham. 1995. *Wildlife and People: The Zimbabwean Success*. New York: Wisdom Foundation.

Glowka, L., F. Burhenne-Guilmin, H. Synge, and others. 1994. *A Guide to the Convention on Biological Diversity*. Environmental Policy and Law Paper no. 30. Geneva: International Union for the Conservation of Nature and World Conservation Union Environmental Law Center.

World Bank and Organisation for Economic Co-operation and Development. 1993. "Environmental Action Programme for Central and Eastern Europe." Document submitted to the Ministerial Conference on Environment for Europe, April 28–30, Lucerne, Switzerland.

World Bank. 1992. *World Development Report 1992*. Washington, D.C.

11

Human Health and the Environment

The environment in which people live greatly influences their health. A degraded environment means a lower quality of life, loss of productivity, and higher health care costs. According to a recent report by the World Health Organization (1997, p. 4).

> Environmental quality is an important direct and indirect determinant of human health; deteriorating environmental conditions are a major contributory factor to poor health and quality of life and hinder sustainable development; poor environmental quality is directly responsible for around 25 percent of all preventable ill-health in the world today, with diarrheal diseases and respiratory infections heading the list.

Those most affected by poor environmental quality are impoverished populations living in rural and peri-urban areas. Of these populations, two-thirds of all ill-health occurs among children. The severity of environmental threats to human health varies from country to country and depends on a number of socioeconomic factors, such as the following:

- Level of education in general and of health education
- Availability of and access to trained nurses and physicians
- Quality of and access to vital services, such as potable water, sanitation, and housing
- Focus of economic activity, for example, agriculture versus industry
- Types of production methods used in these activities, for instance, capital or labor intensive
- Degree of transformation of natural ecosystems.

The environments in which humans live can be divided into the following categories:

- Household environment
- Occupational environment
- Ambient environment.

Each of these environments entails specific threats to human health (table 11.1). Comparing the relative importance of risk factors in each environment can be a useful guide for policymakers attempting to evaluate the most urgent areas for action.

Household Environment

For the poor, the household environment is a major threat to human health. Poor households are characterized by inadequate sanitation and water supply (often compounded by poor hygiene), heavy indoor air pollution, and overcrowding.

The diseases associated with poor household environments occur mainly in developing countries and account for nearly 30 percent of the total burden of disease in the world. Estimates indicate that modest improvements in household environments would eliminate almost 25 percent of this burden, mostly as a result of reductions in diarrheal diseases and respiratory infections. Governments can deploy

---

Based on presentations by Clyde Hertzman.

Table 11.1. *Different Types of Environments and Potential Risks to Human Health*

Type of environment	Risks	Potential effects
Household environment	Poor sanitation Poor water supply Inadequate garbage disposal Indoor air pollution Overcrowding	Infectious diseases Respiratory illnesses Diarrhea Airborne infections
Occupational environment	Exposure to toxic chemicals Noise Stress Debilitating work (for example, agricultural workers, miners, migrant workers, child laborers) Accidents and injuries	Increased risk of chronic disease Morbidity
Ambient environment	Air pollution Water pollution Soil pollution Radiation exposure Disease and pest organisms	Respiratory and cardiorespiratory problems in humans (especially elderly, children, smokers) Neuropsychological damage caused by lead contamination Epidemics and other diseases

Source: Authors.

potent mechanisms to improve this environment by investing in basic education and poverty reduction and by facilitating and stimulating private sector action.

Water and Sanitation

About 1.3 billion people in the developing world lack access to clean, plentiful water. Water quantity is as important as water quality for protecting human health. Without sufficient water in or near the home, proper hygiene, for example, washing hands after defecating and before preparing food, becomes difficult or impossible.

In addition, 2 billion people lack adequate systems for disposing of human wastes, and fecal contamination is a leading cause of disease. Sources can include feces deposited near homes; contaminated drinking water, sometimes caused by poorly designed and/or poorly maintained sewage systems; contaminated fish from polluted rivers and coastal waters; and toxic agricultural products that have been fertilized with human waste or irrigated with water contaminated by such waste.

Diseases transmitted via feces are common in developing countries because of the lack of uncontaminated water supplies and proper sanitation. Figure 11.1 shows the numbers and percentage of population without sanitation or water supply services in different parts of the world.

Indoor Air Pollution

Investigators have identified indoor air pollution as one of the four most critical global environmental problems. People in rural areas of developing countries receive as much as two-thirds of the global exposure to indoor particulates. In some areas, people are exposed to more indoor air pollutants than outdoor air pollutants. Outdoor air in cities such as New Delhi, India, and Xian, China, contains a daily average of

Figure 11.1. Population without Sanitation or Water Supply Services, Selected Countries and Regions, 1990

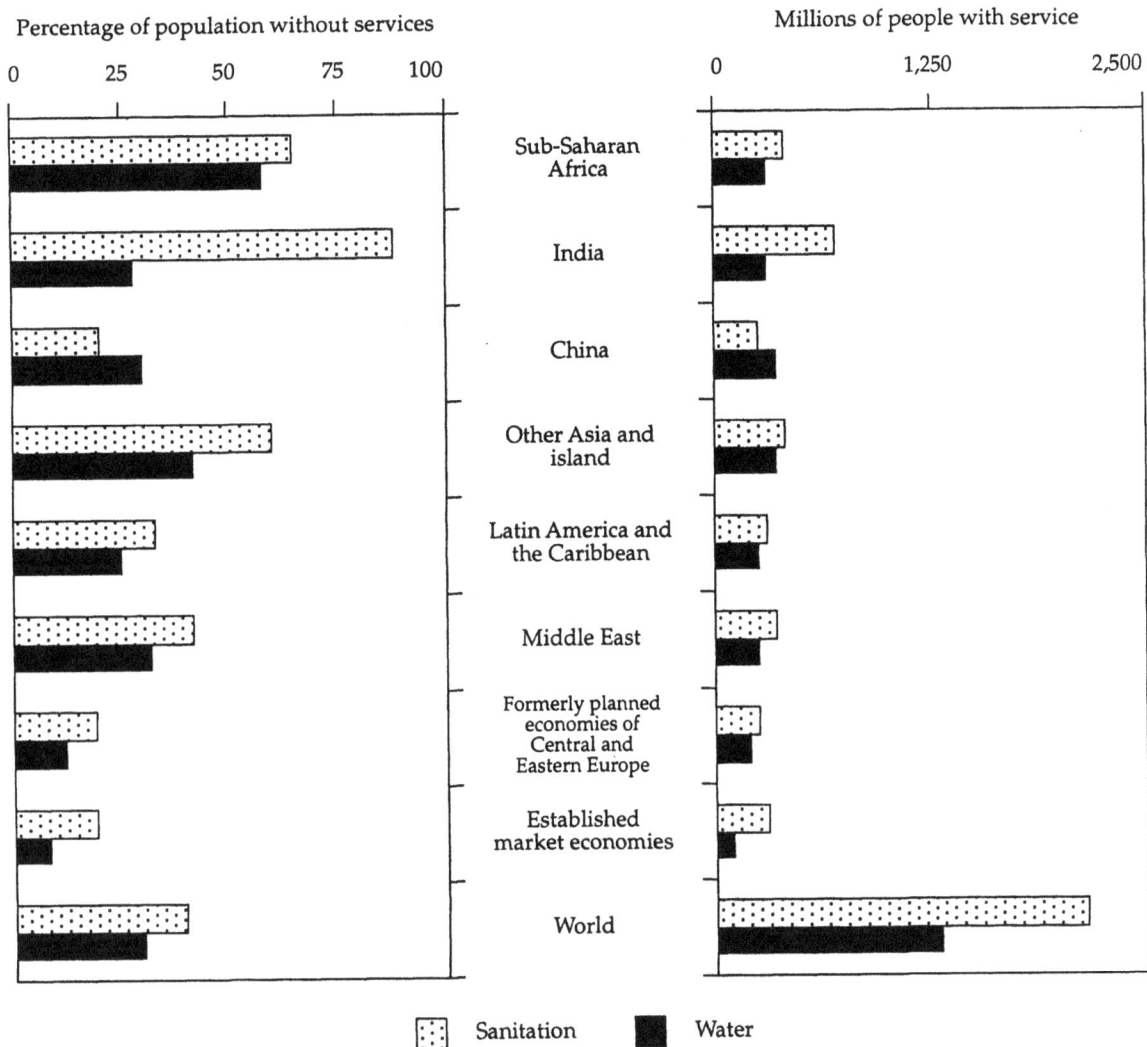

Percentage of population without services

Millions of people with service

0   25   50   75   100

0   1,250   2,500

Sub-Saharan Africa

India

China

Other Asia and island

Latin America and the Caribbean

Middle East

Formerly planned economies of Central and Eastern Europe

Established market economies

World

Sanitation   Water

Note: Coverage is defined in accordance with local standards.
Source: Adapted from World Bank (1993, p. 91).

500 micrograms per cubic meter of total suspended particles. In comparison, smoky houses in Nepal and Papua New Guinea have peak levels of 10,000 micrograms per cubic meter or more of total suspended particulates. The World Health Organization (1997) estimates that as many as a billion people, mostly women and children in developing countries, are exposed to high levels of indoor air pollution.

Overcrowding

Overcrowding is another prevalent problem in developing countries. In many cities 30 to 60 percent of the population live in overcrowded and deteriorating conditions. Overcrowding is associated with increased incidence of airborne infectious diseases, such as influenza. Moreover, poor structures lead to greater exposure to heat, cold, dust, rain, insects, and rodents.

Occupational Environment

The environment in which people work also has a major impact on their health. Each year preventable injuries and deaths in high-risk occupations and chronic illnesses stemming from exposure to toxic chemicals, noise, stress, and physically debilitating work patterns cause 3 percent of the global burden of disease. Agricultural work, in which more than half of all adults in most developing countries are employed, is among the world's most vulnerable occupations. Agricultural workers are exposed to disease-carrying animals and toxic agrochemicals. Miners, construction workers, migrant workers, and child laborers also suffer increased risk of physical injuries and disease because of their occupations.

Ambient Environment

The ambient environment, which is defined as the outdoor environment to which the general public is exposed, includes air, soil, and water. Through these media people may be exposed to various agents that are detrimental to human health, such as germs and other pathogens or toxic substances. Radiation will be dealt with separately.

Air Pollution

People in many cities suffer from the effects of air pollution caused by industry, power plants, road transport, and domestic use of coal. About 1.3 billion residents worldwide are exposed to air pollution levels above recommended limits. Air quality in the industrial countries has generally improved over the past two decades; however, in many developing countries, including the newly industrialized economies of Eastern Europe, air quality has deteriorated. This is due to increased industrial activity, power generation, vehicular traffic, use of leaded fuel in some countries, and poor maintenance of vehicles.

Air pollution damages the human respiratory and cardiorespiratory systems in various ways. The elderly, children, smokers, and those with chronic respiratory difficulties are the most vulnerable. If achievable reductions in urban air pollution could prevent 5 percent of all infections and chronic respiratory diseases, then these reductions could avert 0.6 percent of the global burden of disease (World Bank 1993).

Polluted urban air contains high concentrations of lead, which comes mainly from the exhaust of vehicles burning leaded gasoline. Lead poisons many systems of the body and is particularly damaging to the development of the brain and nervous system in children. Elevated blood levels of lead in children have been associated with impaired neuropsychological development as measured by loss of IQ, poor school performance, and behavioral difficulties.

Water Pollution

Low-, middle-, and high-income countries have polluted and/or are continuing to pollute their rivers, lakes, and coastal waters with a variety of chemical and biological wastes of both industrial and domestic origin. For example, the practice of letting raw wastewater from industry and residential areas flow into rivers or the sea is common. These practices contaminate drinking and irrigation water, affecting fisheries and agriculture.

Investment to prevent runoff into rivers and the sea may be justified purely on economic grounds, even when damage to natural ecosystems is not included. The first justification is the possibility of severe local health consequences. The second is that water resources may become too polluted to use as sources of water supply. This would reduce the number of options available for responding to domestic, agricultural, and industrial demand for water.

Radiation Exposure

Exposure to radiation derives primarily from natural background ionized radiation and radiation used for medical and dental diagnosis. Only a trace amount of additional radiation comes from safely operated nuclear power plants or other installations (roughly 0.001 of the background dose for those living within 50 kilometers of a nuclear power station). However, the risks of nuclear accidents are significant. The consequences of the nuclear power plant accident at Chernobyl, Ukraine, in 1986 have yet to be fully documented, but catastrophic results are already evident. The risk of such accidents is particularly large in the former socialist economies, because of the large number of poorly designed facilities. Standards and safeguards against accidents and occupational hazards have been improved, but risks remain. Related accidents and occupational risks to workers in nuclear industries and to miners of radioactive ores pose serious human health problems.

Measuring and Valuing Environmental Effects on Health

Interest in methods to estimate the burden of ill-health from environmental causes is increasing. One approach uses the unit known as the disability-adjusted life year (DALY). The DALY (see the appendix to this chapter) is a measure that takes into account healthy life years lost from all causes, whether due to premature mortality or as a result of disability (Homedes 1996, p. 1). This measure can be useful for policymakers because it can measure the burden of disease and help identify those interventions that may result in the largest improvement in health.

Valuing environmental impacts on human health can help demonstrate the costs of inaction and be a powerful instrument in promoting changes in government policy and business practices. However, putting a monetary value on the health impacts of pollution presents ethical, theoretical, and practical problems. Some people have moral objections to putting a value on human sickness or mortality. Others argue that accurately assessing the value of health effects from pollution may not be possible.

Considerable uncertainty surrounds the actual identification and measurement of health impacts. Once impacts have been determined, estimating monetary values for associated morbidity (illness) and mortality (death) is often necessary. Figure 11.2 provides an overview of various approaches to valuing environmental impacts on health.

Valuing Mortality

Investigators have used three major approaches for placing monetary values on mortality, namely:

- Willingness to pay approach
- Wage differential approach
- Human capital approach.

WILLINGNESS TO PAY APPROACH. The objective of the willingness to pay method is to estimate how much people are prepared to pay to reduce the likelihood of premature death. The method consists of a survey in which people are asked how much they are prepared to pay for small changes in the risk of death.

An example of the use of the willingness to pay approach was a survey of the number of people in the United States who were prepared to pay to reduce the risk of on-the-job traffic accidents (Dixon 1994). In this study, the estimated value of an annual risk reduction of 0.0001 percent is between US$200 and US$300 per year (in 1986), equivalent to about US$2 million to US$3 million per death avoided. The study presumes that the results also reflect people's willingness to pay for similar reductions in the risk of death from environmental hazards.

Figure 11.2. *Approaches to Valuing the Environmental Impacts on Health*

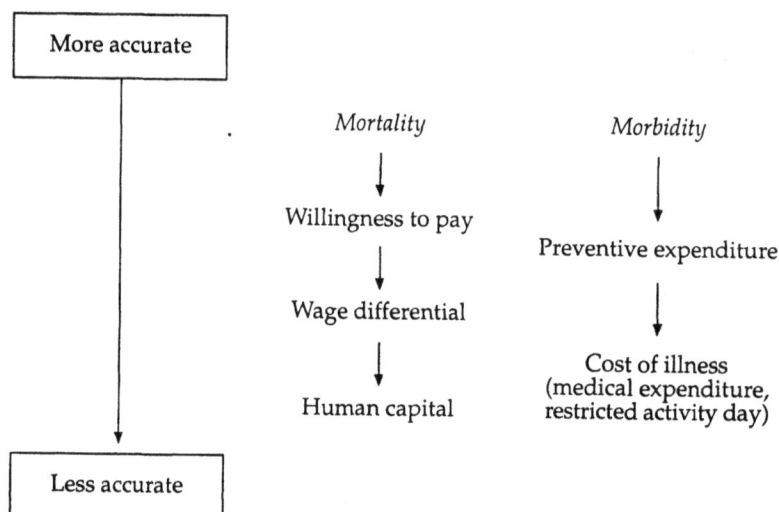

Source: Authors.

WAGE DIFFERENTIAL APPROACH. The wage differential approach is closely related to the willingness to pay approach, but compares differences in wages across a sample of occupations with different annual mortality risks. In this way investigators can establish how much extra compensation is required to induce people to accept slight increases in job risk. Thus it uses differences in wage rates as representative of perceived differences in the chances of dying from occupational hazards.

There are, however, a number of objections to this approach. Perfect information may not be available about the riskiness of a job, and therefore risk factors may not be reflected in wages. In addition, separating the influence of job risk on wages from other factors, such as desirability of the job, may be difficult. Finally, the method assumes that all people have the same attitude toward risk.

A study in the United States using the wage differential approach estimated that the average value to individuals of reducing their mortality risk by 0.0001 is between US$100 and US$800 per year (in 1986 dollars), equivalent to about US$1 million to US$8 million per death avoided (Dixon 1994). Unfortunately, no clear explanation for such a broad range is available.

HUMAN CAPITAL APPROACH. The human capital approach is easy to apply, but is considered to be less accurate and ethically objectionable. It considers individuals as units of human capital that produce goods and services for society. Just as the useful life of manmade capital can be calculated based on expected future production, the human capital approach assumes that the value of each unit of human capital is equivalent to the present value of future output in the form of earnings that might have been generated had the individual not died prematurely. The human capital approach thus values mortality only in terms of wages lost. It does not consider the "human" aspect of mortality, pain, suffering, the intrinsic worth of human life, and a person's noneconomic contributions. In addition, the death of those who are not part of the labor force—such as the aged or infirm—would be without cost according to the human capital approach.

Estimates made using the human capital approach are extremely sensitive to the age of death, income level, skill level, and country of residence. For example, the average cost of the death of a 25-year-old in a country of the Organisation for Economic Co-operation and Development would be estimated at US$2 million to US$5 million, whereas the cost of the death of a person with an equivalent education and job in a poor country could be as little as US$50,000 to US$100,000 (Dixon 1994).

Although the human capital approach grossly underestimates the "worth" of the life of a child, it is sufficient to show the "worth" exceeds the costs of a major immunization program.

Valuing Morbidity

To estimate the cost of morbidity (sickness), investigators can examine both the costs directly associated with the disease, such as for medical care and of lost wages, and what people are prepared to pay to avoid becoming ill from pollution.

COST OF ILLNESS. The direct cost of morbidity can be divided into two categories: the costs of hospital admissions and emergency room visits, that is, medical expenditures for treating illness, and the costs of restricted activity days, that is, days spent in bed, days missed from work, and other days when activities are significantly restricted because of illness. These measures do not include inconvenience, commuting costs, losses in leisure, and other impacts on individuals and their families' well-being, and seriously underestimate or completely ignore the cost of sickness of people who are not members of the labor force. Valuing the costs of morbidity only by lost wages and medical expenditure, while fairly easy to carry out, only indicates the lower bound of the willingness to pay and understates the total cost to individuals.

An example of this method is an estimate of the cost of nonlethal diarrhea in Mexico. In 1990 some 3.4 million people suffered from this condition. Only the costs of treatment and laboratory analysis were considered and for the different age cohorts came to US$30 million, or about US$9 per person (Dixon 1994). Note that this figure represents less than 1 percent of the total cost estimated for deaths from similar causes. By comparison, a study in Brazil estimated the cost of respiratory system diseases by considering only the loss of income due to hospitalization of economically active people, which was taken to represent an estimate of the value of morbidity due to air pollution. However, it ignores the cost of treatment and cost of days missed from work because of sickness.

PREVENTIVE EXPENDITURES. By observing the amounts people living in polluted areas spend on measures to reduce their health risks, investigators can make tentative inferences about the minimum amount they are willing to pay to reduce the risks. The willingness to pay approach is theoretically superior to assessing the costs of illness because it takes into account a broader set of values that an individual places on reducing environmental health risks. However, often people do not have perfect information about the risks related to environmental pollution. Moreover, willingness to pay depends on ability to pay, leading to problems not only for in-country comparisons, but also for cross-country comparisons.

Priority Setting for Policymaking

Policymakers can use these methods to set priorities for action. Investigators should begin by assessing the causes of the greatest damage to human health. By using the three broad categories described in the first section (household environment, occupational environment, and ambient environment), estimating the impact of these environments on human health in terms of morbidity and mortality, and translating this into quantitative information, they can measure the associated monetary losses. With this type of information in hand, policymakers can make well-informed decisions. They should choose policies based on their effectiveness in controlling environmental pollution, the benefits associated with this, and the costs of implementing the measures. In the process, local stakeholders should be involved in identifying key problems and their causes and outlining the extent to which the government and communities can address them.

The above process is difficult and can be side-tracked for a variety of reasons. For example, investment can easily be diverted from one sector to another in response to pressing demands, and thus the major source of pollution may not be addressed. For instance, in some countries, even though poor water supply and sanitation are the largest causes of disease, policy is diverted to other areas, such as reducing air pollution reduction.[1] One reason for this is that air pollution is nonexclusionary, that is, it affects everyone, while access to safe water can be exclusionary, that is, it may affect only certain groups of people. In many developing countries poor neighborhoods lack sanitation and have poor water quality, whereas wealthier neighborhoods may have sewage systems and residents may be able to afford to buy bottled water.

Another example of inappropriate policies are those that do not target the largest offenders within a specific sector. In some cities large industry has been the main source of particulate air pollution, while mobile sources of pollution (automobiles) have caused secondary damage. However, because imposing pollution reduction measures on large industries may be politically difficult, while automobile users generally find organizing themselves to oppose such measures more difficult, policymakers impose stricter standards on automobiles.

These are difficult problems that policymakers need to face, and they should be prepared to make hard decisions. Perhaps with better information about these issues and public awareness of the severity of the problems, the government, private sector, and local communities can take concerted action to reduce some of the key health problems that occur in poor households and occupational and ambient environments.

Conclusion

Many environmental factors affect human health. The potential health effects of a poor environment are infectious diseases, respiratory illnesses, diarrhea, increased risk of chronic disease, and lead-induced neuropsychological damage.

Investigators can use three approaches to determine the environmental costs of ill-health derived from an unhealthy environment: the willingness to pay method, the wage differential approach, and the human capital approach. These controversial approaches attempt to place a value on morbidity and mortality. These general frameworks can form a broad basis for analyzing the health effects of the environment, and often prove useful to policymakers in general terms. Note, however, that these estimates should be considered as representing the lower boundary of the values. If the benefits (although underestimated) of action as calculated in this way outweigh the costs, then the implementation of an environmental improvement project is advised.

In addition, a strong institutional infrastructure is needed to set the rules of the game. It is only when policymakers have such information and have consulted with stakeholders that they can rank actions in order of priority, so that they can start with those that will have the largest impact on improving the population's health. Priority setting involves examining tradeoffs and targeting policy interventions in those areas that most effectively mitigate the adverse health effects of a poor environment.

Appendix: Disability-Adjusted Life Year

The disability-adjusted life year (DALY) is a unit designed to measure the total burden of disease, both as it relates to premature mortality and to disability. Disabilities can be physical or mental. The intended use of the DALY is to help (a) set health service priorities; (b) identify disadvantaged groups and target health interventions; and (c) provide a comparable measure of output for intervention, program, and sector evaluation and planning.

The number of DALYs estimated at any moment reflects the amount of health care already being provided to the population, as well as the effects of all other actions that protect or damage health. Where treatment is possible—whether preventive, curative, or palliative—the effectiveness of the intervention

---

1. In 1992 the World Bank concluded that improving access to clean water and sanitation would be the single most effective means of alleviating human distress. When services were improved in the industrial countries in the 19th and 20th centuries, health improved dramatically (see World Bank 1992).

is the reduction in disease burden that the treatment produces. Effectiveness is measured in the same units (DALYs) as disease burden, and so can be compared across interventions that treat different problems and produce different outcomes. In other words, the DALY can be used to measure the gains in health attributable to different actions.

Table 11.A1 presents estimates in terms of DALYs of the global burden of disease from selected environmental threats as of 1990 and potential worldwide reductions through environmental interventions. It shows clearly that, of the environmental threats shown here, policies aimed at reducing occupational risks, especially accidents, will have the largest influence.

Table 11.A2 presents the estimated burden of disease in poor household environments in demographically developing countries in 1990 and potential reductions achievable through improved household services. Potential health gains from improving the household environment total nearly 80 million DALYs a year in developing countries. The greatest risk reduction will clearly come from addressing causes of diarrhea and respiratory infections.

Other government actions designed to ameliorate unsafe conditions in the work place and pollution of the ambient environment could save 36 million and 8 million DALYs a year, respectively.

Source: Homedes (1996).

References

Dixon, J. 1994. *Economic Toll of Pollution's Effect on Health.* Environment Department Dissemination Notes no. 2. Washington, D.C.: World Bank.

Table 11.A1. *Estimated Global Burden of Disease from Selected Environmental Threats, 1990, and Potential Reductions through Environmental Interventions*

Type of environment and principal related diseases[a]	Burden from these diseases (millions of DALYs per year)	Reduction achievable through feasible interventions[b] (percent)	Burden averted by feasible interventions (millions of DALYs per year)	Burden averted per 1,000 population (DALYs per year)
Occupational	318	—	36	7.1
Cancers	79	5	4	0.8
Neuropsychiatric	93	5	5	0.9
Chronic respiratory	47	5	2	1.8
Musculoskeletal	18	50	9	3.1
Accidental injury	n.a.	81[c]	20	16.0
Urban air	170	n.a.	8	1.7
Respiratory infections	123	5	6	1.2
Chronic respiratory	47	5	2	0.5
Road transport (major vehicle injuries)	32	20	6	1.2
Total	473[d]	—	50	10.0

— Not available.

n.a. Not applicable.

a. The diseases shown are those for which there is substantial evidence of a relationship with the particular environment.

b. Estimates derived from the product of the efficacy of the interventions and the proportion of the global burden of disease that occurs among the exposed. All estimates of efficacy are speculative and assume the implementation of known, feasible, and affordable interventions in the circumstances encountered in developing countries.

c. Computed by subtracting motor vehicle injuries (32 million DALYs) from all accidental injuries (113 million DALYs).

d. Adjusted for double counting.

Source: World Bank (1993, p. 95).

Table 11.A2. Estimated Burden of Disease from Poor Household Environments in Demographically Developing Countries, 1990, and Potential Reduction through Improved Household Services

Principal diseases related to poor household environments[a]	Relevant environmental problem(s)	Burden from these diseases in developing countries (millions of DALYs per year)	Reduction achievable through feasible intervention (percent)[b]	Burden averted by feasible interventions (millions of DALYs per year)	Burden averted per 1,000 population (DALYs per year)
Tuberculosis	Crowding	46	10	5	1.2
Diarrhea[c]	Sanitation, water supply, hygiene	99	40	40	9.7
Trachoma	Water supply, hygiene	3	30	1	0.3
Tropical cluster[d]	Sanitation, garbage disposal, vector breeding around the home	8	30	2	0.5
Intestinal worms	Sanitation, water supply, hygiene	18	40	7	1.7
Respiratory infections	Indoor air pollution, crowding	119	15	18	4.4
Chronic respiratory diseases	Indoor air pollution	41	.15	6	1.5
Respiratory tract cancers	Indoor air pollution	4	10[e]	...	0.1
Total		338	n.a.	79	19.4

n.a. Not applicable.

... Negligible.

Note: The demographically developing group consists of Sub-Saharan Africa, India, China, other Asian islands, Latin America and the Caribbean, and the Middle East.

a. The diseases listed are those for which there is substantial evidence of a relationship with the household environment.

b. Estimates derived from the product of the efficacy of the interventions and the proportion of the burden of disease that occurs among the exposed. The efficacy estimates assume the implementation of improvements in sanitation, water supply, hygiene, drainage, garbage disposal, indoor air pollution, and overcrowding of the kind being made in poor communities in developing countries.

c. Includes diarrhea, dysentery, cholera, and typhoid.

d. Diseases within the tropical cluster most affected by the domestic environment are schistosomiasis, South American trypanosomiasis, and bancroftian filariasis.

e. Based on inadequate data on efficacy.

Source: World Bank (1993, p. 90).

Homedes, Nuria. 1996. "The Disability-Adjusted Life Year (DALY): Definition, Measurement, and Potential Use." Human Capital Development Working Papers. World Bank, Washington, D.C.

World Bank. 1992. *World Development Report 1992*. New York: Oxford University Press.

_____. 1993. *World Development Report 1993*. New York: Oxford University Press.

World Health Organization. 1997. *Health and the Environment in Sustainable Development: Five Years after Rio*. Geneva.

Other Recommended Readings

Beaglehole, B., R. Bonita, and T. Kjellstroem. 1993. *Basic Epidemiology*. Geneva: World Health Organization.

Hertzman, Clyde. 1995. "Environment and Health in Central and Eastern Europe." A report for the Environmental Action Programme for Central and Eastern Europe. Submitted to the World Bank, Washington, D.C.

World Health Organization. 1990. *Public Health Impacts of Pesticides Used in Agriculture*. Geneva.

_____. 1994. *Anthology on Women, Health, and Environment*. Geneva.

_____. 1996. *World Health Report*. Geneva.

World Resources Institute. 1996. *World Resources 1996–97*. New York: Oxford University Press.

12

Planning and Environmental Indicators

In every stage of planning, information and knowledge are essential, particularly during the initial phases, when problems are identified and priorities chosen. Naturally, a range of other factors—apart from information—also influences policy choices, such as political and economic realities, values, and institutional and cultural frameworks. The combination of these factors greatly affects policy decisions. Nevertheless, an accurate information base can facilitate sensible decisionmaking.

In the area of the environment and sustainable development, decisionmakers have faced considerable difficulties because of inadequate information, particularly in developing countries. As Agenda 21 noted in 1992:

> The gap in the availability, quality, coherence, standardization and accessibility of data between the developed and the developing world has been increasing, seriously impairing the capacities of countries to make informed decisions concerning environment and development (UNCED 1992, chapter 40, p. 4).

In many instances primary data are lacking. In others, abundant data and information may be available at the national and international levels that is inaccessible to planners at the local level. For instance, agencies and institutions may have different objectives for data collection and therefore use different collection, classification, and analytical methods. In these cases data coordination, compilation, and harmonization are generally needed. Another constraint is the possible absence of a culture of disseminating information widely and publicly (Winograd 1995).

Measuring Progress toward Sustainability

The essential connections between the environment and development have gained universal acceptance. New research and knowledge must focus on collecting and integrating information to reflect the goals of sustainable development. Indicators are needed that reflect the goals of sustainable development more accurately, particularly indicators that are cross-disciplinary, for instance, ecological-economic, socioeconomic, and socioecological (figure 12.1).

Traditional indicators, such as national accounting figures, for instance, gross national product, do not include environmental dimensions, and thus cannot be used as measures of progress toward sustainability. Some countries are moving toward green accounting, such as France and Norway; however, these initiatives are in a developmental stage and are not yet available for cross-country comparisons. Genuine savings (see chapter 4) is also a move in this direction.

The United Nations and the multilateral development banks have compiled indicators that can be used for cross-country comparisons, such as deforestation rates, particulate air pollution (for some industrial countries), or carbon dioxide emissions from industrial processes. Nonetheless, their use tends to be limited to a small number of countries (World Bank 1997). The United Nations Development Programme and other international and regional institutions compile social indicators or human development indicators, and collect information on such issues as demographic, health, education, violence,

---

Based on presentations by M. Winograd and J. Dixon.

Figure 12.1.   *Indicators to Meet the Challenges of Sustainable Development*

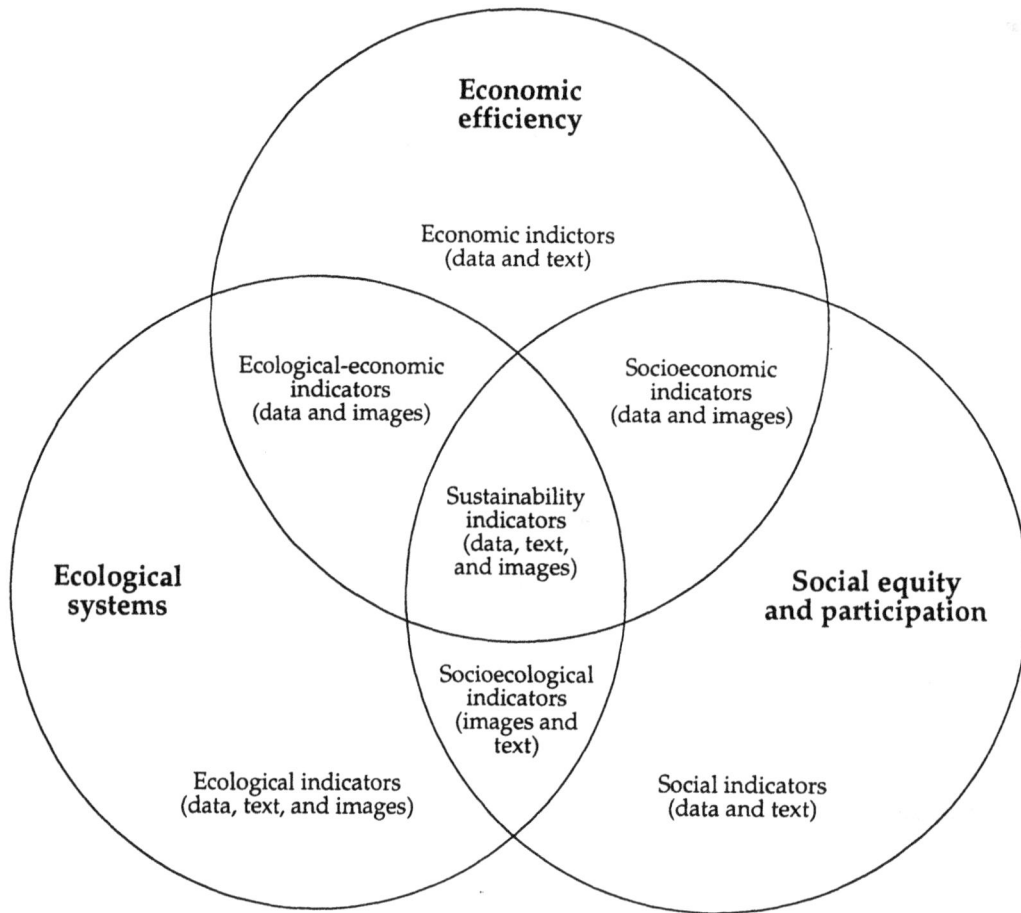

Source: Adapted from Winograd (1997).

and crime trends. These examples represent only initial attempts at compiling information for sustainable development, and much needs to be done to increase coordination among those collecting environmental, social, and economic data to help facilitate the assessment of the interaction and relationships between these sectors.

While indicators serve a number of purposes, in general they help

- Prioritize areas of action
- Catalyze increased awareness about environmental issues among the public at large
- Monitor and evaluate progress in managing natural resources
- Monitor and evaluate progress on environmental policy
- Monitor and evaluate social and economic trends in general.

Table 12.1 illustrates the scales and uses of indicators of environmental information. Depending on the environmental issue and the use of the indicator, information can be compiled in different ways. In many cases, simple indicators can be developed, which greatly enhances the information base from which decisions can be made on national and local levels. Once such a base exists, it facilitates the construction of indexes or aggregated indicators on national, regional, and global levels.

Table 12.1.   *Scales and Uses of Indicators*

Category	Global	Regional	National	Local
Environmental issue	Global climate change	Regional climate change	Emissions due to changes in land use and energy consumption	Deforestation, energy consumption
Indicators	Indexes	• Indexes • Aggregated indicators	• Indexes • Aggregated indicators • Simple indicators	• Simple indicators
Uses	Follow-up; negotiations and formulation of policies and actions	Identification and action on prioritized policies and actions	Definition and implementation of strategies, policies, and actions	Application, analysis, and implementation of policies and actions

Source: Winograd (1997).

Indicators

With regard to ecology and sustainable development, it is often scientists who identify and define problems and provide decisionmakers and the public with important findings. Because of the complexity of the issues, simplification is needed to understand and apply scientific knowledge to design and execute practical solutions. One way in which this information can be simplified is by designing environmental indicators.

Indicators are summarized using aggregated data, selected and transformed from primary data sets. Aggregations can be made to various degrees (figure 12.2). First, primary data are collected from, for example, environmental monitoring programs, and analyzed. A selection of analyzed data can be chosen to represent the entire data set and can be used as simple indicators. Sometimes combining many sets of primary data into one single composite indicator or index is possible. For example, the human development index, mentioned earlier uses this approach.[1]

An environmental example to illustrate these different levels of aggregations is measures of greenhouse gas emissions. Direct measures of emissions of gases like carbon dioxide and methane would represent primary data. Each of these gases affects the possibility of global warming to different degrees, depending on the duration of their presence in the atmosphere and their capacity to absorb the heat radiated by the earth. For each gas these two factors are combined to calculate the global warming potential (analyzed data). The global warming potential then constitutes the weighting factors for the contribution of each particular gas to the greenhouse effect. This weighting factor is multiplied by a country's emissions of each gas expressed in carbon dioxide equivalents (simple indicator). From here, all emissions can be calculated to make a composite indicator or index for one country's contribution to climate change.

The next step is to decide on the types of indicators that should be designed first. The most common framework is the pressure-state-response framework (figure 12.3). This framework is constructed to indicate the chain of causality between human activities and environmental degradation. Human activities

---

1. The index was designed to capture as many aspects of human development as possible into a composite index of achievements in basic human capabilities in three fundamental dimensions: a long, healthy life; knowledge; and a decent standard of living (see United National Development Programme 1996, p. 28).

Figure 12.2.   Aggregation of Data

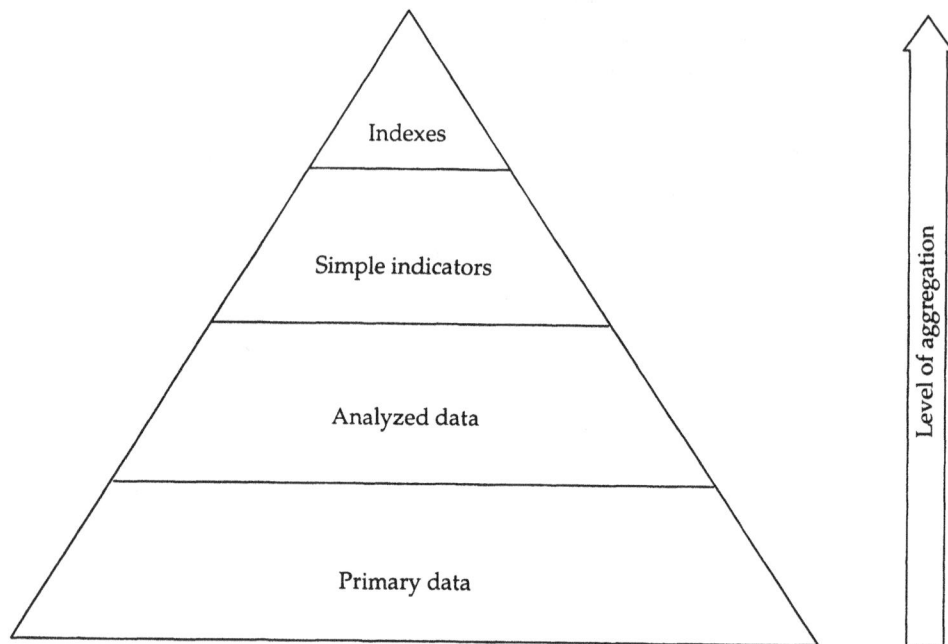

Source: Authors.

Figure 12.3.   Pressure-State-Response Framework

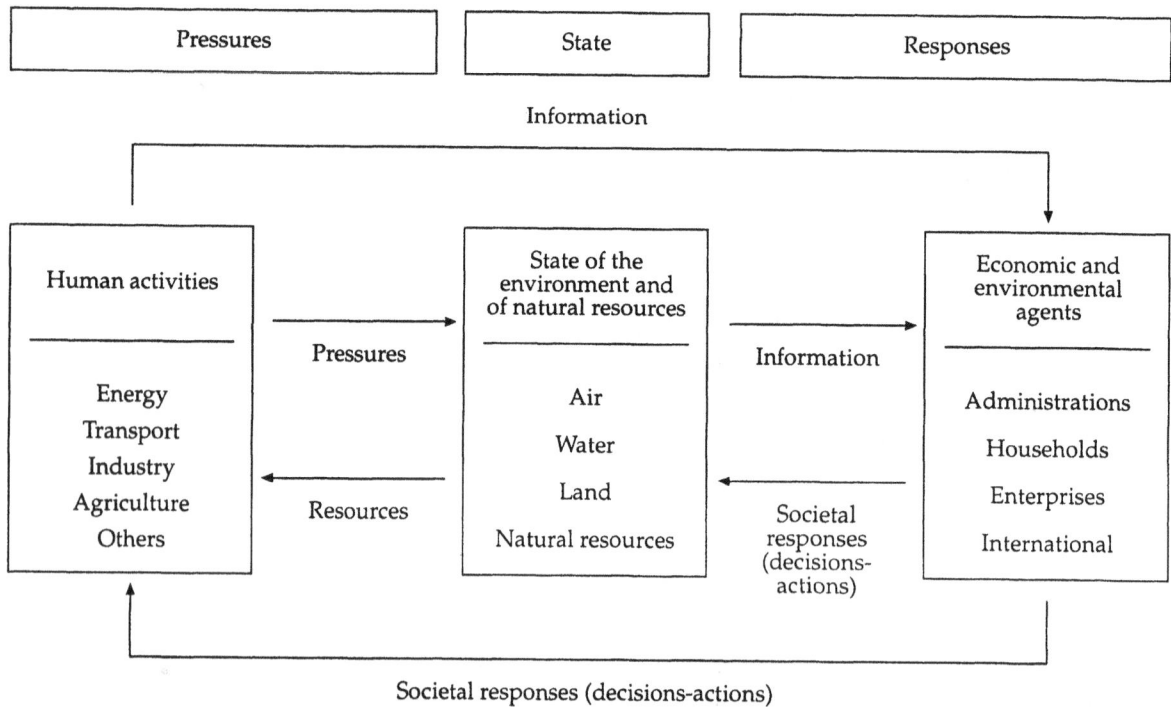

Source: Hammond and others (1994).

act as driving forces or pressures on the environment. For example, intensive agriculture without techniques to stop erosion can cause land degradation, thus the quality or state of the environment changes. In response to such changes society may initiate different kinds of actions, such as a policy aimed at disseminating knowledge about erosion protection measures to farmers. Indicators can be divided as pressure, state, or response indicators depending on the information they are designed to provide.

Note that the pressure-state-response model is only a taxonomic model that permits classifying and organizing the information, and is not a causal model. To convert the model to a causal-effect model, its categories need to be expanded, and other tools, such as geographic information systems, need to be included to account for the spatial and temporal dimensions. In addition, the different components and relationships between development and the environment would need to be integrated into the model.

Information Requirements

The types of basic data required to develop indicators vary in scope and character. All data need to fulfill the requirements of timeliness, reliability, and usefulness (Winograd 1995). Note that information may be used in different forms, for instance, numerical and graphic data or qualitative texts in cases where capturing the information in numbers, tables, or images is not possible. Even if uncertainties about data quality persist, such as the underlying assumptions for data assembly, crude indicators can provide useful information.

Countries need different types of indicators because of their unique social and cultural perspectives and developmental stages. The Organisation for Economic Co-operation and Development has developed criteria for selecting indicators (box 12.1). At the local level, the presence or absence of a particular

---

Box 12.1. *Criteria for Indicator Selection*

Policy relevance and utility for users

An environmental indicator should

- Provide a representative picture of environmental conditions, pressure on the environment, or society's response
- Be simple, easy to interpret, and able to show trends over time
- Be responsive to changes in the environment and to related human activities
- Provide a basis for international comparisons
- Be either national in scope or applicable to regional environmental issues of national significance
- Have a target or threshold against which to compare it so that users can assess the significance of the values associated with it.

Analytical soundness

An environmental indicator should

- Be theoretically well founded in technical and scientific terms
- Be based on international standards and international consensus about its validity
- Lend itself to be linked to economic models, forecasting systems, and information systems.

Measurability

The data required to support the indicator should be

- Readily available or made available at a reasonable cost-benefit ratio
- Adequately documented and of known quality
- Updated at regular intervals in accordance with reliable procedures.

indicator species may be enough to guide the village to scrutinize its changes in land use.[2] At the national level, aggregated indexes of biodiversity loss in specific ecosystems may elicit discussions on new land tenure arrangements. At the global level, the rate of tropical deforestation may influence such actions as the drafting of international agreements and declarations.

Temporal and Spatial Dimensions of Indicators

Because of scientific discoveries and increased economic activity, the relationship between socioeconomic systems and the environment has changed dramatically. Figure 12.4 illustrates some of the trends of evolving environmental problems that extend over spatial and temporal dimensions. For example, in the 1960s the emphasis as concerned environmental problems was on problems of a direct, short-term nature, such as the effects of industrial pollution in the form of air particulates. These types of problems tended to be of a short-term nature and were confined within national boundaries. Recent scientific work has underlined the transboundary and global effects of environmental pollution (see chapter 10).

In addition to these dimensions, environmental damage has become more complex. In the developing world, nonpoint sources are the largest contributor to pollution. Pollution from large industries, one of the primary sources of pollution in the 1960s in the industrial countries, pales in comparison to that of motorized scooters in urban areas, chemical inputs in agriculture, and dispersed small-scale industries such as tanneries and textile factories. Because of the increasing scope and disparate nature

Figure 12.4.   The Changing Nature of Environmental Problems

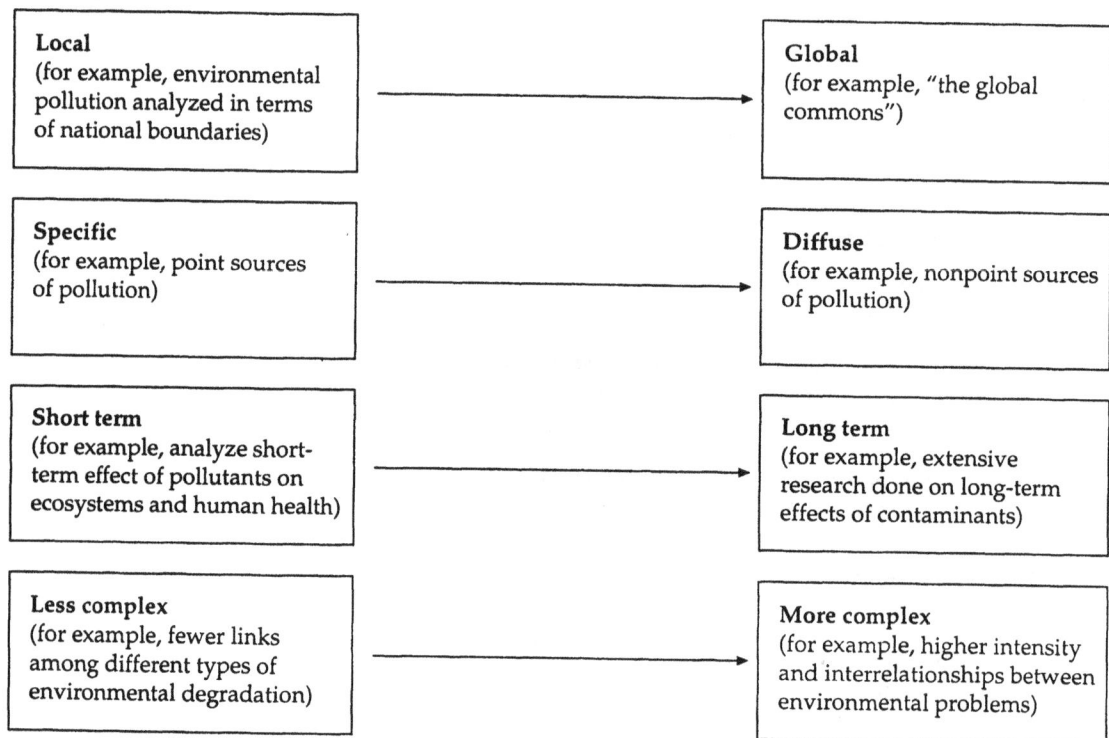

Local
(for example, environmental pollution analyzed in terms of national boundaries) → Global
(for example, "the global commons")

Specific
(for example, point sources of pollution) → Diffuse
(for example, nonpoint sources of pollution)

Short term
(for example, analyze short-term effect of pollutants on ecosystems and human health) → Long term
(for example, extensive research done on long-term effects of contaminants)

Less complex
(for example, fewer links among different types of environmental degradation) → More complex
(for example, higher intensity and interrelationships between environmental problems)

Source: Adapted from Winograd (1997).

---

2. An indicator species is one that flags changes in biotic or abiotic conditions. Its status provides information about the overall condition of the ecosystem and of other species in that ecosystem.

of these problems, more aggregated indicators need to be designed for policymakers to be able to make informed decisions.

International and National Projects to Develop Indicators

In response to the identified need for more useful information, Agenda 21 encourages governments, international organizations, and nongovernmental institutions to develop and use indicators for sustainable development (UNCED 1992). At the international level, the Commission on Sustainable Development has adopted a work program that includes developing an initial set of 130 indicators and devising methodology sheets for each of these indicators (see the appendix to this chapter for an example of these and a selection of the list of indicators). The purpose of this extensive list is to allow countries to compile and use a subset of indicators that depends on each country's national priorities, goals, and targets. Over time, indicators that show links between the social, economic, and environmental sectors will be developed and become more highly aggregated to reflect the links among ecological systems, social equity and participation, and economic efficiency (figure 12.1).

Agenda 21 urged countries to "carry out inventories of environmental, resource and developmental data, based on national/global priorities for the management of sustainable development...and to determine the gaps and organize activities to fill those gaps" (UNCED 1992, chapter 40, para. 8). Pursuing these objectives can be done at different levels according to resources and needs. The starting point can be an inventory of the use of available country data. From here, the data gaps and needs can be assessed to strengthen the existing base. To be efficient and cost-effective, the collection of new data must be preceded by a thorough cross-sectoral process of clarifying priorities for sustainable development. The identification of indicators can then serve as a tool for both decisionmaking and for monitoring the efficiency of policy responses for mitigating negative environmental impacts. Throughout this process, one agency should become the focal point for coordinating the integration of economic, social, and environmental data. Many institutions could be involved in producing data and submitting it to this focal point. Such a procedure would permit harmonization of collection, compilation, production, distribution, and dissemination methods (Winograd 1995).

Conclusion

Accurate information about ecological systems, economic efficiency, and levels of social equity and participation are the building blocks for developing effective policy for sustainable development. This type of information is not only necessary for policymakers, but also for civil society and the private sector. If increased, accurate empirical and quantitative data were available on sustainability, the state, the private sector, and individuals could make better informed decisions about resource allocation.

Information must be built on a strong base of primary data, analyzed data, simple indicators, and if possible, indexes. Currently enormous gaps exist in data compilation, information is seldom cross-disciplinary, and data rarely reflect relationships between environmental and socioeconomic dimensions. Moreover, the tasks of collection and compilation have become onerous because of the increasing complexity of environmental issues caused by an intensification of economic activity and production processes, and as scientific discoveries reveal the complexity of ecological systems.

With this in mind, countries need to set priorities for collecting relevant data that could eventually be fed into aggregated indexes. They can do so by using the pressure-state-response framework to analyze those areas subject to the most intense pressures. Further analysis is then necessary to develop an indicator. This entire process will be more effective if a single agency acts as the coordinating point, so that information is properly and efficiently collected, compiled, and disseminated.

Improved indicators for environmental sustainability enhance decisionmaking at all levels. Improved collection, compilation, access to, and dissemination of information about socioeconomic systems and the environment can significantly change how people perceive problems, and can thereby result in more effective and creative problem solving.

Appendix: Sustainable Use of Natural Resources in Mountain Areas

Category: Environmental

In an effort to both promote sustainable development and standardize methods for its evaluation, the United Nations has developed a set of 130 indicators for different aspects of sustainable development. To facilitate their use as well as test their effectiveness, a methodology sheet is available for each indicator. Below is a sample methodology sheet for measuring the sustainable use of natural resources in mountain areas. It may be used as a guide for compiling data on land and resource use in mountainous regions.

1. Indicator

    (a) Name: Qualitative assessment of the condition and level of sustainable use of natural resources in mountain areas.
    (b) Brief Definition: This indicator is a composite of four sub-indexes which describe in broad terms the state or condition of the natural resource base in a mountain area: namely (i) the extent of protection of soil; (ii) the area of hazard zones; (iii) the extent of degraded areas; and (iv) a measure of productivity.
    (c) Unit of Measurement: The first three indicators above relate to land use or misuse and can be measured in hectares of land area and expressed as the percentage of a mountain area. The forth indicator measures yields of natural resource products (fuelwood, timber, wildlife food, non-wood forest products, etc.) which can be expressed in dollars, grain equivalent unit, or other values and compared to the replacement of these products in terms of reproduction and growth.

2. Placement in the Framework

    (a) Agenda 21: Chapter 13: Managing Fragile Ecosystems: Sustainable Mountain Development.
    (b) Type of Indicator: State.

3. Significance (Policy Relevance)

    (a) Purpose: This indicator assesses the condition or degree of stability, which can be a clue of probable sustainability of natural resource uses in mountain areas. Another purpose of the indicator is to identify obvious land degradation and misuses that need policy responses, in order for mountains to be returned to sustainable use.
    (b) Relevance to Sustainable/Unsustainable Development: A natural resource base in a well-managed, protected, and productive state has a better potential for sustainable use than a deteriorating or already degraded base. The sustainable development of mountain ecosystems must be based on land uses for which mountains have a comparative advantage and which are compatible with long-term productivity in fragile upland ecosystems. This indicator relates directly to the land capability or suitability of the areas, since land uses exceeding the carrying capacity of an area are not sustainable. For example, land uses related to parks, eco-tourism, harvesting non-wood products from forests, biological preserves, etc. are often sustainable uses in mountain areas, whereas cultivation on steep slopes without extra-ordinary conservation measures, or building housing in landslide hazard areas are not sustainable.

    The indicator provides an approximation to determine if the land can potentially provide for adequate livelihood for the local people without degrading the natural resource base. Having information, at least an overview, on the status of land and resource use is the first step relevant to policy decisions related to fighting poverty in mountain areas, for land use planning, and overall rural development. Such a database is also essential for policy decisions on infrastructures, disaster planning, and economic development in mountain areas.

(c) Linkages to Other Indicators: This indicator has close association with several other environmental indicators pertaining to Chapters 10, 11, 13, and 15 of Agenda 21. These would include: land use change, land condition change, protected forest area as a percent of total forest area, population change in mountain areas, and protected areas as a percent of total area. In addition, the indicator is generally linked to other socioeconomic and institutional measures, such as population density and sustainable development strategies.

(d) Targets: Chapter 13 of Agenda 21 establishes objectives for sustainable development related to land productivity and appropriate use. The indicator is suitable for the setting of local targets. In some cases, it can relate to national targets for forestry and land use.

(e) International Conventions and Agreements: The Convention on Biological Diversity and the International Decade for Natural Disaster Reduction apply to this indicator.

4. Methodological Description and Underlying Definitions

(a) Underlying Definitions and Concepts: An actual measurement of sustainability of natural resource use is at best difficult. It requires a good data base and at least several growing seasons to measure. The indicator, therefore, is a simple measure of the probability of general sustainability in a mountain area. Many countries already have programs for land-use assessment, forest assessment, soil inventory, and other monitoring and inventory data that can be used in this index.

In general terms mountains are extensive physiographic features which demonstrate clear altitudinal features in climate, soil, or natural vegetation, with high mountains being above the natural timber line. Mountain ecosystems include mountain basins, valleys, and high volcanic ring plains and high plateau, as well as the mountains themselves. As the indicator is further refined, the more precise definition of mountains, hills, and related terms will follow FAO's Global and National Soils and Terrain Digital Databases (SOTER) procedures, which define various land forms in terms of slopes and relief intensity.

(b) Measurement Methods: For the sub-indexes on soil protection, hazard zones, and degraded areas, many of the measurements of vegetation, soils, and land uses are standard procedures which draw on sources such as remote sensing, existing maps, geographic information system (GIS) databases, field observations, etc. to assess land use conditions. Forest assessment data and soil surveys, for example, may be used. Some of the measurements, such as identification of landslide hazard areas are somewhat more specific, but use the same measurement techniques. The sub-index on productivity takes volumetric units for yields of natural resource products (fuelwood, timber, wildlife food, non-wood forest products, etc.). This may also be converted to a standard unit of value, for example, to dollars or a grain equivalent type unit.

To calculate the composite indicator, rate the four components descriptions below for a mountain area, such as a watershed, and summarize the four scores for a combined index from 0 to 400.

(i) Soil Protection: Score approximate percentage of mountain area where this statement generally applies:

Protection against accelerated erosion is good in terms of adequate vegetative cover in forests, rangelands, parks, preserves or other wildlands; conservation practices in agricultural or agro-forestry areas protect soil from accelerated water and wind erosion.

_____%

(ii) Hazard Areas: Score approximate percentage of mountain area where this statement does not apply:

Potential unstable hazard areas exist where risk is high for landslides, avalanches, mud-flows, wildfires, volcanic effects, flooding, and other hazards that endanger people and inhibit development in such areas.

_____%

(iii) Degraded Areas: Score approximate percentage of mountain area where this statement does not apply:

Degraded areas exist where the production of natural resource goods and development are obviously restricted and include: areas of accelerated surface erosion; zones with vegetation degraded by overgrazing; areas of chemical or other contamination; fire impacted areas; areas where some non-productive vegetation dominates; zones where water supply is now restricted from, for example, salt-water encroachment, ground water contamination, etc.; and saline areas.

_____%

(iv) Evidence of Productivity: Score approximate percentage of mountain area where this statement applies:

For wildlands and rangelands: productivity or yields of timber, plants, fuelwood, wildlife meat, beef, and other products is sustainable in that present use approximately equals the replacement of these goods by reproduction and growth and the resource base is not being destroyed.

For small-scale agricultural and agro-forestry areas: levels of agricultural yields can probably continue approximately at present levels with the same farming practices and inputs (as opposed to situations where crop productivity is obviously declining due to excessive soil losses or other reasons).

For water: water use can continue at approximately present demand levels or additional water can be imported (as opposed to situations where ground-water mining, salt encroachment, contaminants, or other impacts threaten water supplies; or where the available water supply is generally restricted).

_____%

Index Total (0-400%) _____%

(c) The Indicator in the DSR Framework: Within the DSR Framework, this is a State indicator of land use and condition.

(d) Limitations of the Indicator: Often data are not readily available for mountain areas and may need to be collected. Productivity is a complex measurement to standardize. Surveys for productivity, if based on interviews, are subject to bias. The rationale for this index and its aggregation has its limitations and may not apply to all countries. Attempts to extrapolate data into mountain areas are not advisable. Hazard zones, such as landslide areas, require techniques specific to mountain areas.

(e) Alternative Definitions: Not available.

5. Assessment of the Availability of Data from International and National Sources

(a) Data Needed to Compile the Indicator: Land use, forest, and range assessment data, such as vegetation, erosion, sedimentation, overgrazed and burned areas, contaminated lands, water resources, and hazard areas, are required. The data should be compatible with the United Nations Food and Agriculture Organization's (FAO) Global Forest Resource Assessment methods to facilitate data sharing.

(b) Data Availability: In some countries, a data base will be available for mountain areas, but often these are the zones least well assessed. Remote sensing and GIS will be important tools for many of the areas.

(c) Data Sources: National data sources can be based on remote sensing data; field observations; interviews; agriculture census; existing surveys, maps and available reports; economic studies.

6. Agencies Involved in the Development of the Indicator

The lead agency for the development of this indicator is the United Nations Food and Agriculture Organization (FAO). The contact point is the Assistant Director General, Sustainable Development Department, FAO; fax no. (39-6) 5225 3152.

7. Further Information

(a) Further Readings:
A discussion document on this indicator will result from the third annual inter-agency meeting on Chapter 13, April 1996.

(b) Other Contacts:
International Centre for Integrated Mountain Development (ICIMOD).
Consortium for Sustainable Andean Development (CONDESAN).
The Mountain Institute within the Mountain Forum.
LEAD AGENCY: FAO

Source: UNCED (1992).

References

Hammond, A. L., and others. 1994. *Environmental Indicators: A Systematic Approach to Measuring and Reporting on Environmental Policy Performance in the Context of Sustainable Development.* Washington, D.C.: World Resources Institute.

UNCED (United Nations Conference on Environment and Development). 1992. *Agenda 21: Programme of Action for Sustainable Development.* New York: United Nations.

United Nations Development Programme. 1996. *Human Development Report 1996.* New York: Oxford University Press.

Winograd, E. 1995. *Environmental Indicators for Latin America and the Caribbean: Toward Land-Use Sustainability.* Washington, D.C.: Inter-American Institute for Co-operation in Agriculture, Deutsche Geseltschaft für Technische Zusammenarbeit, Organization of American States, and World Resources Institute.

Winograd. M., and others. 1997. "Marco Conceptual Para un Sistema de Indicadores de Gestion y Planificacion Ambiental." Cali, Colombia: CIAT-PNUMA and UPA-DNP.

World Bank. 1997. *World Development Indicators.* Washington, D.C.

Other Recommended Readings

Bakkes J. A., G. van den Born, J. Helder, R. Swart, C. Hope, and J. Parker. 1994. "An Overview of Environmental Indicators: State of the Art and Perspectives." Environment Assessment Technical Reports. Rijksinstituut voor Volksgezondheid en Milieuhygiëne, Cambridge University, and United Nations Environment Programme. United Nations Environment Programme, Environmental Assessment Subprogramme, Nairobi.

Bossel H. 1999. "Indicators for Sustainable Development: Theory, Method, Application." Report to the Balaton Group. International Institute for Sustainable Development, Winnipeg, Canada.

Centro Internacional de Agricultura Tropical, World Bank, and United Nations Environment Programme. 1999. *Rural Sustainability Indicators: Outlook for Central America.* http://www.ciat.cgiar.org/indicators/index.htm

Hardi P., and T. Zdan, eds. 1997. *Assessing Sustainable Development: Principles in Practice.* Winnipeg, Canada: International Institute for Sustainable Development.

Moldan B., and S. Billharz, eds. 1997. *Sustainability Indicators: Report of the Project on Indicators of Sustainable Development.* New York: John Wiley.

Organisation for Economic Co-operation and Development. 1993. *OECD Core Set of Indicators for Environmental Performance Reviews*. Environment Monographs no. 83. Paris.

Scientific Committee on Problems of the Environment (SCOPE). 1995. *Indicators of Sustainable Development for Decisionmaking*. Report of the Workshop of Ghent. Brussels: Federal Planning Office of Belgium.

Statistical Office of the European Communities. 1999. Information about European Commission initiatives and European Union policies in general. http://www.europa.eu.int/

United Nations Department for Policy Coordination and Sustainable Development. 1996. *Indicators of Sustainable Development: Framework and Methodologies*. New York: United Nations.

Verbruggen, Harmen, and Huib M. A. Jansen. 1995. "International Coordination of Environmental Policies." In Henk Folmer, H. Landis Gabel, and Hans Opschoor, eds., *Principles of Environmental and Resource Economics*. Cheltenham, U.K.: Edward Elgar.

Winograd, M. 1997. "Horizontal and Vertical Linkages in the Context of Sustainable Developent Indicators." In B. Moldan and S. Billharz, eds., *Indicators of Sustainable Development*. New York: John Wiley.

Winograd M., and J. Eade. 1997. *Environmental and Sustainability Indicators for Latin America and the Caribbean: The Use of GIS (Geographic Information Systems)*. In B. Moldan and S. Billharz, eds., *Indicators of Sustainable Development*. New York: John Wiley.

Winograd M., A. Farrow, and J. Eade. 1998. *Atlas de Indicadores Ambientales y de Sustentabilidad para America Latina y el Caribe: ATLAS CD*. CD-ROM, version 1. Cali, Colombia: Centro Internacional de Agricultura Tropical and Programa de las Naciones Unidas para el Medio Ambiente.

Winograd M., N. Fernandez, and A. Farrow. 1998. *Tools for Making Decisions in Latin America and the Caribbean: Environmental Indicators and Geographical Information Systems*. Cali, Colombia: Centro Internacional de Agricultura Tropical and Programa de las Naciones Unidas para el Medio Ambiente.

World Bank. 1995. "Monitoring Environmental Progress, A Report on Work in Progress." Environmentally Sustainable Development Department, Washington, D.C.

_____. 1997. *Expanding the Measure of Wealth: Indicators of Environmentally Sustainable Development*. Environmentally Sustainable Development Studies and Monographs no. 17. Washington, D.C.: Environment Department.

_____. 1998. *World Development Indicators 1998*. Washington, D.C.